FUN *with* FAT QUARTERS

Nancy J. Martin

That Patchwork Place®

Contents

Dedication

To Cleo Nollette—a true friend, who not only helps me pick up the scattered pieces left by my harried lifestyle but also helps me cut, piece, and quilt all those fabric pieces that are such an important part of my life.

Acknowledgments

Grateful thanks are extended to the following people, whose generous help made this book possible:

Marta Estes, for help with the organization and miscellaneous details;
Monica Doramus, for entering into the computer the manuscript of this computer-illiterate author;
Roxanne Carter, for machine quilting several small quilts;
Judy Eide, Donna Gundlach, Teresa Haskins, Beverly Payne, Nancy Sweeney, and Sue Von Jentzen for their fine hand quilting;
All of my beginning students, whose eager enthusiasm and myriad questions inspired this book;
And a special thank you to Delberta Murray and Julie Stewart at Keepsake Cottage Fabrics in Bothell, Washington, for the generous loan of fabric bolts and fat quarters.

Credits

Editor-in-Chief . . . . Barbara Weiland
Technical Editor . . . . Ursula Reikes
Managing Editor . . . . Greg Sharp
Copy Editor . . . . Liz McGehee
Proofreader . . . . Tina Cook
Text and Cover Design . . . . . Joanne Lauterjung
Typesetting . . . . Joanne Lauterjung
Photography . . . . Brent Kane
Illustration and Graphics . . . . Laurel Strand

Fun with Fat Quarters ©
© 1994 by Nancy J. Martin
That Patchwork Place, Inc., PO Box 118, Bothell, WA 98041-0118 USA

Printed in the United States of America
99 98 97 96 95 94   6 5 4 3 2 1

Martin, Nancy J.
    Fun with fat quarters / Nancy J. Martin
        p. cm.
    ISBN 1-56477-042-7
    1. Quilting—Patterns. 2. Patchwork—Patterns. I. Title.
TT835.M8293 1994
    746.9'7—dc20   93-33013
                                                          CIP

How often seemingly ordinary events influence other aspects of our lives. Such was the case when I began forming my ideas for *Fun with Fat Quarters.*

When I rearranged my fabric library, I was amazed at the number of coordinated packs of fat quarters that I had purchased. These pieces of fabric measure 18" x 22" rather than the standard quarter yards that are cut selvage to selvage and measure 9" x 44". There were Liberty of London™ prints purchased in Australia and reproduction chintzes from the Netherlands. I always seem to collect fabrics, rather than teacups or souvenir plates, as I travel. In addition, there were those irresistible packs of fat quarters found in local quilt shops and at quilt shows. One group of fat quarters, a recent birthday present, was still folded inside a half-pint basket and tied with ribbon.

In speaking with other quilters, I found the compulsion to purchase these packets of fat quarters was quite common. The color-coordinated packs helped in making fabric selections. Fat quarters selected from a basket on the counter were easier to match to other fabric and eliminated carrying heavy bolts of fabric around the store. Yet very few of these fabrics ever found their way into quilts. Although the fabric was color coordinated, there was rarely enough fabric to make a sizable wall hanging. Also, very few quilt patterns were geared to the use of fat quarters.

Another event influenced my writing. My husband began to make his very first quilt. He has a logical, analytical mind that always needs to know "why" for each step of the process. His eager questions recalled those myriad questions often asked by beginning quilters.

A short time later, I taught several beginning quilt classes, something I had not done for a number of years. To share the enthusiasm of beginning quilters as they successfully complete their first projects is its own reward for a quilt teacher. But I was doubly rewarded, for my students' most common questions became the focus of my "Tips from the Teacher."

Throughout the book, these questions can be found inside a shaded box. A clear, thorough answer is given along with carefully illustrated drawings. These Tips from the Teacher will provide you with the same helpful hints and information that you would receive in my class or workshop to ensure a successful project.

Thus, *Fun with Fat Quarters* fills two basic needs: an easy-to-use book for beginning quilters and a book written with quilts and fabric requirements geared to fat quarters. The quilts are quick and easy to piece, so quilters of all abilities will appreciate these projects when they need to piece a special project on short notice. The rotary cutting and speed piecing will leave you more time to lavish on a special hand-quilted border design.

So gather together your bundles of fat quarters, read the section entitled "How to Use This Book," select one of the ten quilt designs, grab your rotary cutter, and have fun with fat quarters!

Essential Ingredients

Rotary Cutter and Mat

A large rotary cutter enables you to quickly cut strips and pieces without templates. A cutting mat is essential to protect both the blade and table on which you are cutting. An 18" x 24" mat allows you to cut long straight or bias strips. You might also consider purchasing a smaller mat to use when you are working with scraps.

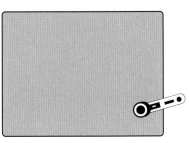

Cutting mat

Rotary-Cutting Rulers

Use a "see-through" ruler to measure and guide the rotary cutter. There are many appropriate rulers on the market, but my favorite is the Rotary Rule™. It is made from ⅛" clear Plexiglas and includes markings for 45° and 60° angles, guidelines for cutting strips, plus the standard measurements. The Rotary Mate™ is a 12"-long ruler with the same features. Both of these rulers are marked with large, clear numbers and do not have a lot of confusing lines.

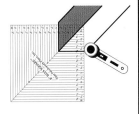

The Bias Square® is critical for cutting accurate bias squares. This acrylic ruler is available in three sizes: 4", 6", or 8" square, and is ruled with ⅛" markings. It features a diagonal line, which is placed on the bias seam, enabling you to cut two accurately sewn half-square triangles.

The Bias Square is also convenient to use when cutting small quilt pieces, such as squares, rectangles, and triangles. The larger 8" size is ideal for quick-cutting blocks that require large squares and triangles as well as making diagonal cuts for half-square and quarter-square triangles. A 20cm-square metric version is available for those who work with metric measurements.

If the Bias Square is unavailable, you can adapt a general-purpose rotary ruler to work in a similar fashion.

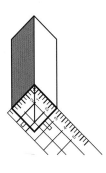

1. Make a template by cutting a square of see-through plastic in the size specified for the bias square in the quilt directions.
2. Draw a diagonal line on the template, bisecting the square.
3. Tape the template onto the corner of an acrylic ruler.
4. Follow the cutting directions given for the quilt you are making, substituting the template-adapted corner of the ruler for the Bias Square.
5. You will need to make a new template for each size bias square required for the quilt you are making. The most common sizes of bias squares required are 2", 2½", and 3".

Sewing Machine

Stitching quilts on a sewing machine is easy and enjoyable. Spend some time getting to know your machine and become comfortable with its use. Keep your machine dust-free and well oiled.

Machine piecing does not require an elaborate sewing machine. All you need is a straight-stitch machine in good working order. It should make an evenly locked straight stitch that looks the same on both sides of the seam. The tension should be adjusted so you can produce smooth, even seams. A puckered seam causes the fabric to curve, distorting the size and shape of the piecing and the quilt you are making.

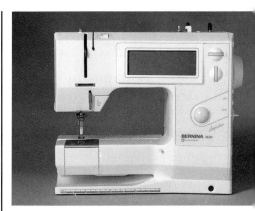

Pins

A good supply of glass- or plastic-headed pins is necessary. Long pins are especially helpful when pinning thick layers together.

If you plan to machine quilt, you will need to hold the layers of the quilt together with a large supply of rustproof, size 2 safety pins.

Iron and Ironing Board

Frequent and careful pressing is necessary to ensure a smooth, accurately stitched quilt top. Place your iron and ironing board, along with a plastic spray bottle of water, close to your sewing machine.

Needles

Use sewing-machine needles sized for cotton fabrics (size 70/10 or 80/12). You will also need hand-sewing needles (Sharps) and hand-quilting needles (Betweens #8, #9, #10).

TIPS

from the Teacher

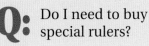

Q: Do I need to buy special rulers?

A: It is possible to cut quilt pieces with any see-through ruler that you have, and you can also adapt a general purpose ruler to cut bias squares. However, it is easier to use the special rulers that I recommend. They contain only the necessary cutting lines and strategic alignment guides to help keep the fabric grain line in the correct position. Since you don't have to visually screen out unnecessary lines, your eyes can quickly focus on only the lines you need. Using a specialized ruler improves cutting accuracy, makes your quiltmaking experience more fun, and frees you from the matching and stitching frustrations that can result from inaccurate cuts.

If these rulers are not available at your local quilt or fabric shop, they can be ordered from That Patchwork Place, Inc., P.O. Box 118, Bothell, WA, 98041-0118.

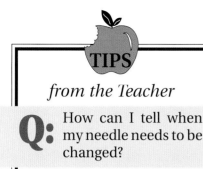
Q: How can I tell when my needle needs to be changed?

A: If you hear a popping sound as the needle enters your fabric, the needle is dull. Change to a new needle to avoid unsightly snags or thread pulls in your fabric.

Scissors

Use good-quality shears for cutting fabric only. Thread snips or embroidery scissors are handy for clipping stray threads.

Seam Ripper

This little tool will come in handy if you find it necessary to remove a seam before resewing.

Fabric Selection

Some quilt patterns in this book call for an assortment of light and dark fabrics, others for a combination of lights, accents, and darks. Your fabric and color choices will depend on what appeals to you or what is available in your scrap bag or collection of fat quarters. Because you may be working with scraps or fat quarters, you may be using a number of different fabrics to represent a single value. When cutting the pieces shown as "dark" in the quilt plan, for example, you can use two, three, or ten different dark fabrics. These might be all the same color (like an assortment of dark blues) or different colors of the same value (like a combination of dark blues, dark greens, and browns).

If you are having trouble deciding on a color scheme, select a bundle of fat quarters that has been color coordinated. Often this can be the basis for an effective color scheme with the purchase of additional background fabric. You can also purchase more of a particular fabric that you wish to predominate in your quilt. For instance, if the fabric requirements call for six dark fat quarters, you can purchase three fat quarters of a red print that you really like and one each of three other red print fat quarters.

Many of the quilts shown in this book do not use a single light print as a background print but a combination of fabrics that are similar in color and value. Study the differences in these quilts and see which you prefer. If you prefer the look of a single light background fabric, convert yardage given in fat quarters to yards. To do so, divide the number of fat quarters by four. For example, 14 fat quarters would be equal to purchasing 3½ yards of fabric.

For best results, select lightweight, closely woven, 100% cotton fabrics. Polyester content may make small patchwork pieces difficult to cut and sew accurately.

Yardage Requirements

As a quilting teacher, I have often seen the problems created by purchasing too little fabric. There is no flexibility to make the quilt bigger, to make a mistake, or to change your mind. So, the fabric requirements given in this book are generous and are based on yardage that is 42" wide after prewashing. If your fabric is wider than 42", there will be a little left over at the end of your strips. If your fabric is narrower than 42", you may need to cut an extra strip. Save any extra yardage or strips for future scrap quilts.

Many of the yardage amounts specify fat quarters. This is an 18" x 22" piece of fabric rather than the standard quarter yard that is cut selvage to selvage and measures 9" x 44". The fat quarter is a more convenient size to use, especially when cutting bias strips for bias squares. Shops offer the added convenience of fat quarters already cut and bundled. Look for the basket or bin of fat quarters when selecting fabrics.

A: Wash all fabrics first to preshrink, test for colorfastness, and get rid of excess dye. Continue to wash fabric until the rinse water is completely clear. Add a square of white fabric to each washing of the fabric. When this white fabric remains its original color, the fabric is colorfast. A cupful of vinegar in the rinse water may also be used to help set difficult dyes.

After washing, press fabric and fold into fourths lengthwise. Make straight cuts with the rotary cutter across each end. When using the length of fabric, make straight cuts from one end and bias cuts from the other end. Then, fold the fabric to store it.

Make it a habit to wash and prepare fabrics after they are purchased. Then, your fabric will be ready to sew when you are.

TIPS

from the Teacher

Q: Should I wash my fabric before using it?

Rotary-Cutting Tips

The Importance of Grain Lines

Fabric is made of threads (technically called yarns) that are woven together at right angles. This gives fabric the ability to stretch or remain stable, depending on the grain line that you are using. The lengthwise grain runs parallel to the selvage and has very little stretch, while the crosswise grain runs from selvage to selvage and has some "give" to it. All other grains are considered bias. A true bias is a grain line that runs at a 45° angle to the lengthwise and crosswise grains.

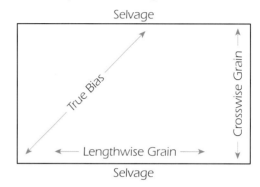

In most cases, the rotary-cutting directions use the following guides for grain-line placement:

1. All strips are cut on the crosswise grain of fabric.
2. Squares and rectangles are cut on the lengthwise and crosswise grains of fabric.
3. Half-square triangles are cut with the short sides on the straight grain and the long side on the bias. The bias square technique produces sewn half-square triangles whose grain lines follow this guideline.
4. Quarter-square triangles have the short sides on the bias and the long side on the straight grain. They are generally used along the outside edges of the quilt where the long edge will not stretch.
5. The straight grain of fabric should fall on the outside edge of all pieced blocks.

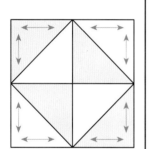

Envelope Block

TIPS

from the Teacher

Q: How can I straighten a fabric that is not printed correctly on the grain?

A: If fabric is badly off grain, pull diagonally to straighten as shown. It is impossible to rotary-cut fabrics exactly on the straight grain of fabric since many fabrics are printed off grain. In rotary cutting, straight, even cuts are made as close to the grain as possible. A slight variation from the grain will not alter your project.

Cutting Straight Strips

Rotary cutting squares, rectangles, and other fabric shapes begins with cutting strips of fabric. These strips are then crosscut to the proper dimensions and angles. All strip measurements include ¼"-wide seam allowances.

To cut strips from the crosswise grain:

1. Fold and press the fabric with selvages matching, aligning the crosswise and lengthwise grains as much as possible. Place the folded fabric on the rotary-cutting mat, with the folded edge closest to your body. Align the Bias Square with the fold of the fabric and place a cutting ruler to the left as shown.

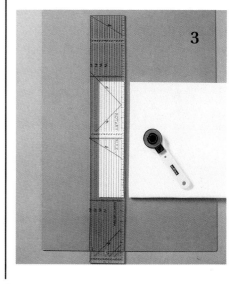

2. Remove the Bias Square and make a rotary cut along the right side of the ruler to square up the edge of the fabric. Hold the ruler down with your left hand, placing the smallest finger off the edge of the ruler to serve as an anchor and prevent slipping. Stand comfortably, with your head and body centered over your cutting. Do not twist your body or arm into an awkward position.

   As you cut, carefully reposition your hand on the ruler to make sure the ruler doesn't shift and the markings remain accurately placed. Use firm, even pressure as you cut. Begin rolling the cutter on the mat before you reach the folded fabric edge and continue across. For safety's sake, always roll the cutter away from you. Remember that the blade is very sharp, so be careful!

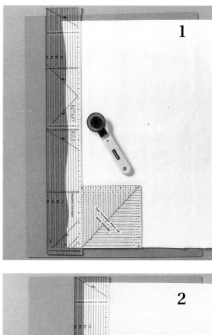

3. Fold fabric again so that you will be cutting four layers at a time. Cut strips of fabric, aligning the clean-cut edge of the fabric with the ruler markings at the desired width. Open the fabric strips periodically to make sure you are cutting straight strips. If the strips are not straight, use the Bias Square to realign the ruler on the folded fabric and make a fresh cut as in step 2 to square up the edge of the fabric before cutting additional strips. Don't worry. This adjustment is common!

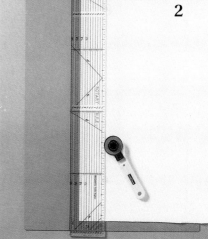

Q: Is a rotary cutter safe to use?

A: A rotary cutter has a *very sharp* blade. It is so sharp that you can cut yourself without even knowing it. If you are not extremely careful, you can also cut other people and objects that you had no intention of slicing. Before you begin rotary cutting for the first time, it is important to know some simple safety rules.

1. Close the rotary cutter safety shield when not in use.
2. Roll the cutter away from yourself. Plan the cutting so your fingers, hands, and arms are never at risk.
3. Keep the cutter out of the reach of children.
4. Dispose of used blades in a responsible manner. Wrap and tape cardboard around them before placing them in the garbage.

For comfort's sake, think about your posture and the table height as you cut. Stand to cut—you'll have more control than when sitting. Many quilters find they are more comfortable and can work longer if the cutting table is higher than a normal sewing table so they don't have to bend as they cut. If you work on a table in the center of the room, you can easily walk to another side of the table to make your next cut, rather than moving the fabric or the cutting mat.

Q: What do I do if I'm left-handed?

A: If you are left-handed, reverse all directions. Begin by placing the fabric to your left and the ruler to your right. Use a mirror to view the photos. This will help you see the proper cutting alignment.

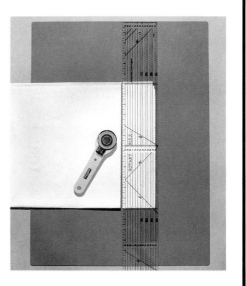

Q: How do I clean my rotary cutter?

A: Remove the lint that builds up between the blade and the front sheath of your rotary cutter. Dismantle the cutter, paying careful attention to how the pieces go together. Carefully wipe the blade with a soft, clean cloth, adding a very small drop of sewing-machine oil to the blade where it lies under the front sheath. Try this first, *before* changing to a new blade when the cutting action seems dull.

Squares and Rectangles

1. Cut fabric into strips the measurement of the finished square, plus seam allowances.
2. Using the Bias Square, align top and bottom edges of strip and cut fabric into squares the width of the strip.
3. Cut rectangles in the same manner. First use the shorter measurement of the rectangle to cut strips, then use the longer measurement to cut the strips into rectangles.

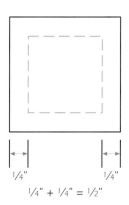

¼" + ¼" = ½"

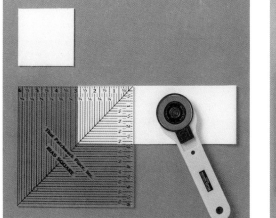

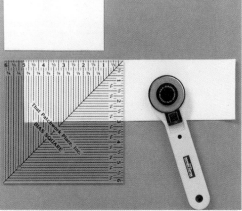

4. To cut a small, odd-sized square or rectangle for which there is no marking on your cutting guide, make an accurate paper template (including ¼" seam allowances). Tape it to the bottom of the Bias Square and you will have the correct alignment for cutting strips or squares.

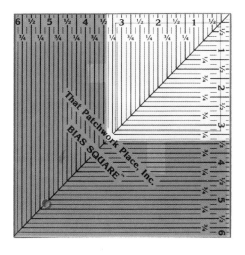

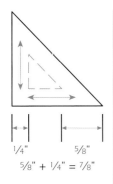

Half-Square Triangles

Most of the triangles used in the quilts in this book are half-square triangles. These triangles are cut so that the straight grain is on the short edges of the triangle. Cut a square ⅞" larger than the finished size of the short edge of the triangle to allow for seam allowances; then cut the square once diagonally to yield two half-square triangles.

1. Cut a strip the desired finished measurement, plus ⅞".
2. Cut the strip into squares, the same measurement as the strip width.
3. Cut a stack of squares once diagonally.

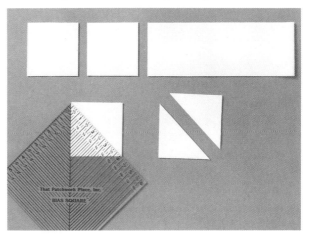

Nubbing Corners on Half-Square Triangles

Nubbing the corners on half-square triangles makes it easier to match edges precisely. Use the Bias Square to trim the corners. The example shown here is a half-square triangle with a finished dimension of 4".

1. To quick-cut this triangle, cut a 4⅞" square of fabric and cut it once diagonally.
2. To trim the corners, add ½" to the finished size of the short side. Position the 4½" mark on the Bias Square on the fabric triangle as shown. The points of the triangle will extend ⅜". Trim them off with the rotary cutter.

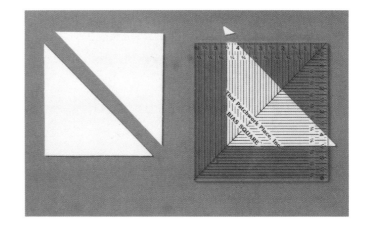

Quarter-Square Triangles

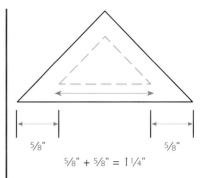

These triangles are cut so that the straight grain is on the long edges of the triangles. Then the long sides are placed along the outside edges of blocks and quilts to keep the edges of your quilt from stretching. Cut a square 1¼" larger than the finished size of the long edge of the triangle; then cut it twice diagonally to yield four quarter-square triangles.

1. Cut a strip the desired finished measurement, plus 1¼".
2. Cut the strip into squares, the same measurement as the strip width.
3. Cut a stack of squares twice diagonally.

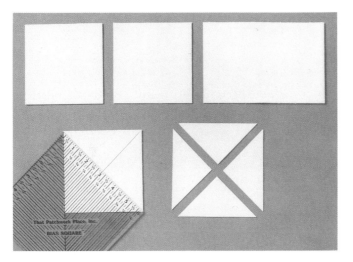

Strip Piecing

Many of the quilts in this book contain simple units based on a Four Patch or Ninepatch. Strip piecing is a quick and easy way to mass produce these units. It eliminates the long and tedious repetition of sewing together individual pieces.

To make Four Patch or Ninepatch units, first cut strips across the crosswise grain of fabric as shown on page 9. Cut these strips in half at the fold, to get two 21" strips. Longer strips have a tendency to bow or gather when sewn. Cutting the strips in half also gives you a greater variety of fabric combinations for scrappy quilts.

To determine the width to cut strips, add a ¼"-wide seam allowance to each side of the finished dimension on the desired shape. For example, if the finished dimension of a square will be 2", cut 2½"-wide strips. Strip widths given for all quilts include ¼"-wide seam allowances on each side.

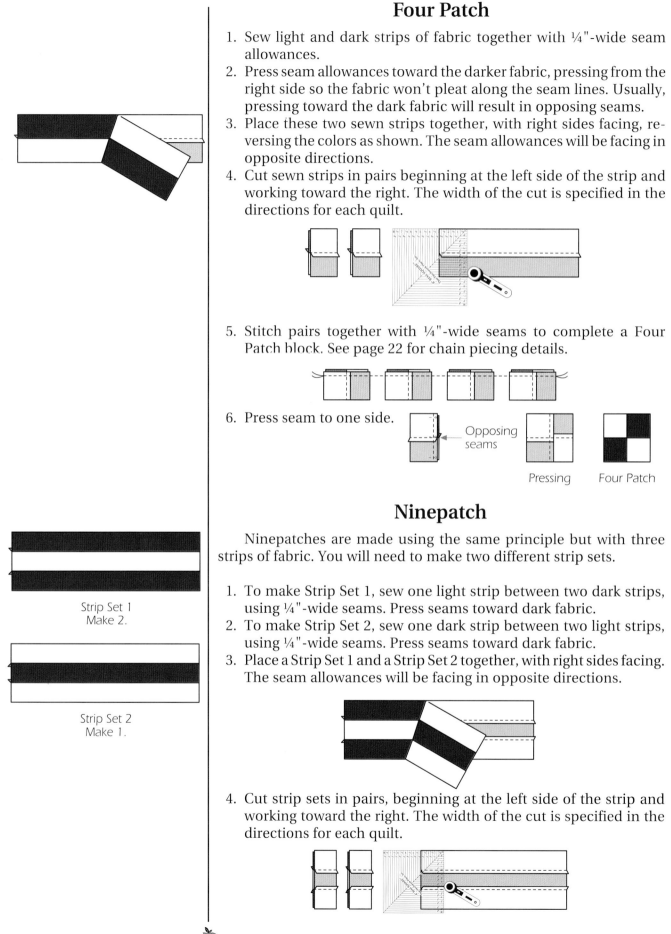

Four Patch

1. Sew light and dark strips of fabric together with ¼"-wide seam allowances.
2. Press seam allowances toward the darker fabric, pressing from the right side so the fabric won't pleat along the seam lines. Usually, pressing toward the dark fabric will result in opposing seams.
3. Place these two sewn strips together, with right sides facing, reversing the colors as shown. The seam allowances will be facing in opposite directions.
4. Cut sewn strips in pairs beginning at the left side of the strip and working toward the right. The width of the cut is specified in the directions for each quilt.

5. Stitch pairs together with ¼"-wide seams to complete a Four Patch block. See page 22 for chain piecing details.

6. Press seam to one side.

Opposing seams

Pressing   Four Patch

Ninepatch

Ninepatches are made using the same principle but with three strips of fabric. You will need to make two different strip sets.

1. To make Strip Set 1, sew one light strip between two dark strips, using ¼"-wide seams. Press seams toward dark fabric.
2. To make Strip Set 2, sew one dark strip between two light strips, using ¼"-wide seams. Press seams toward dark fabric.
3. Place a Strip Set 1 and a Strip Set 2 together, with right sides facing. The seam allowances will be facing in opposite directions.

4. Cut strip sets in pairs, beginning at the left side of the strip and working toward the right. The width of the cut is specified in the directions for each quilt.

Strip Set 1
Make 2.

Strip Set 2
Make 1.

5. Stitch pairs together with ¼"-wide seams. See page 22 for chain-piecing details.

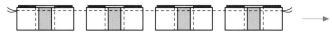

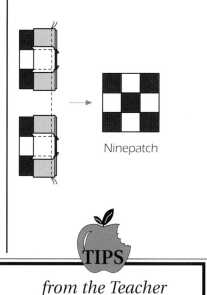

Ninepatch

6. Cut remaining Strip Set 1 into the same width pieces as the pairs.
7. Stitch remaining pieces to previously sewn pairs to complete the Ninepatch blocks.
8. Press seams as shown.

Pressing

TIPS
from the Teacher

Q: Quilt names are confusing to me. Why will one quilt have different names for the block, set, and completed quilt?

A: Blocks made from traditional quilt patterns are the foundation or building blocks used to make a quilt top. Most of these patterns have one or more commonly accepted names. Since the block shown below has two Four Patch units, I call it Double Four Patch.

The Double Four Patch blocks are set together in a traditional design called Barn Raising. This set is most often used for Log Cabin blocks but can be used for any block that contrasts light and dark fabrics. In a Barn Raising set, the pattern begins in the center and continues to radiate in bands of light and dark fabrics to the corners of the quilt.

The name of the completed quilt is chosen by the maker and need not correspond to or contain the traditional quilt pattern name. The quilt pictured on page 31 was named Vintage Barn Raising because it features reproduction prints of old fabrics.

Cutting Bias Strips

Cut bias strips for bias squares and binding as follows:

1. Align the 45° marking of the ruler along the selvage and make a bias cut.
2. Measure the width of the strip from the cut edge of the fabric. Cut along the edge of the ruler.

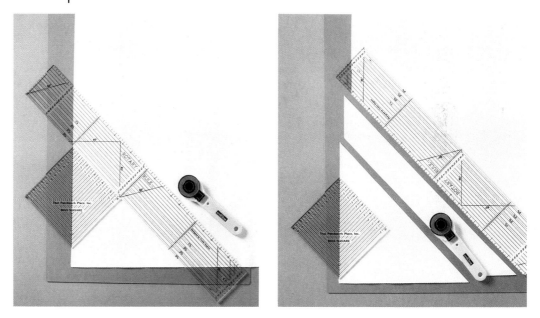

TIPS
from the Teacher

Q: What do I do if my ruler is too short to cut bias strips?

A: When cutting fat quarters into bias strips, a 24"-long ruler is too short for several of the cuts. After making several cuts, carefully fold the fabric over itself so that the bias edges are even. Continue to cut bias strips. As you near the end of the fat quarter, unfold the fabric to make the final cuts.

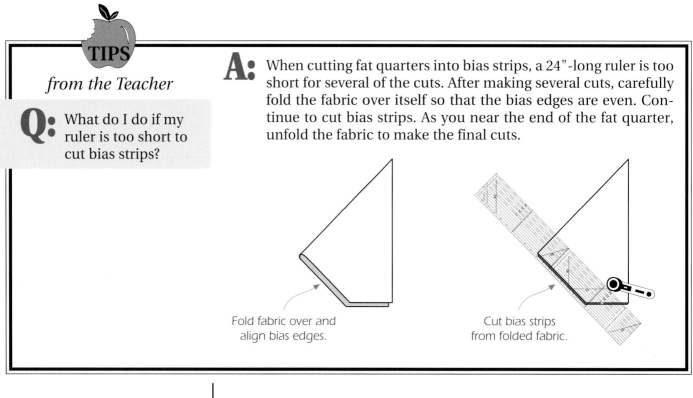

Fold fabric over and align bias edges.

Cut bias strips from folded fabric.

Making Bias Squares

Many traditional quilt patterns contain squares made from two contrasting half-square triangles. The short sides of the triangles are on the straight grain of fabric while the long sides are on the bias. These are called bias-square units. Using a bias strip-piecing method, you can easily sew and cut bias squares in many sizes. This technique is especially useful for small bias squares, where pressing after stitching usually distorts the shape (and sometimes burns fingers).

Cutting Small Amounts of Bias Squares

1. To make fabric more manageable, cut two fat quarters (18" x 22") of contrasting fabric and layer with right sides facing up. You will cut bias strips from both fabrics at the same time.

2. Use the 45° line on the Bias Square ruler to locate the true bias and then use a longer ruler to make a bias cut. The cutting chart will tell you how far from the corner to make your first bias cut. In most cases, you will cut strips the same width as the bias squares you will cut. For example, cut bias strips 2½" wide for 2½" cut bias squares. After piecing, you will have 2" finished bias squares. This is an easy general rule to remember, but specific strip widths are provided with the quilt directions.

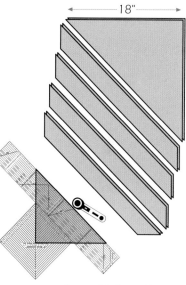

Layer fabrics with right sides up.

3. Sew the strips together, with right sides facing, on the long bias edge with ¼"-wide seams, offsetting the edges ¼" as shown. Press seams toward the darker fabric. (If cutting bias squares 1¼" or smaller, you may want to press the seams open to evenly distribute the fabric bulk.)

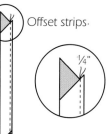

Offset strips.

¼"

NOTE: Each bias square will require two cuts. The first cut is along the side and top edge. It removes the bias square from the rest of the fabric and is slightly larger than the correct size. The second cut along the remaining two sides again aligns the diagonal and trims the bias square to the correct size.

4. Align the 45° mark of the Bias Square ruler with the seam line. Cut first two sides. Turn the strip. Align the 45° mark with the seam line, and the cut edges of the strip with the desired measurement of the unfinished bias square; cut the third and fourth sides.

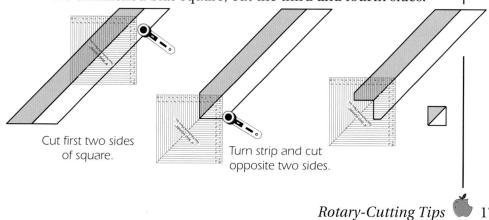

Cut first two sides of square.

Turn strip and cut opposite two sides.

5. Align the 45° mark on the Bias Square ruler with the seam line before cutting the next bias square.

> **NOTE:** All directions in this book give cut size for bias squares; finished size after stitching will be ½" smaller.

Cutting Large Amounts of Bias Squares

For several of the quilts in this book, you will need to cut a sizable amount of bias squares. Use the technique shown below to help conserve time and fabric. Remember, all strips are cut from fat quarters (18" x 22") of fabric. The directions specify the fabrics to use and the width of the strips to cut.

1. Layer two fat quarters of fabric, with right sides facing up, and cut as shown on page 17. The cutting chart below lists the distance from the corner for the first cut.
2. Arrange the strips in the order you are to sew them. Beginning in the corner, select a strip from the top layer. Then select the strip next to it from the bottom layer. Continue to select strips in this manner, alternating from the top and bottom layers as you move toward the opposite corner of the strips. This will give you two sets of strips to sew together. See illustrations on page 19.
3. Sew strips together along the bias edges. Try to keep the left edge and lower edge aligned evenly as you sew. To do so, offset the edges as shown when sewing strips together.

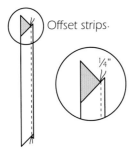
Offset strips.
¼"

Fat Quarters Cutting Chart for Bias Squares

Based on 1 light and 1 dark fat quarter (18" x 22") of fabric.

Distance from Corner for First Cut	Strip Width	Cut Size of Bias Square	Yield	Finished Size of Bias Square
2½"	* 1¾"	1½"	176	1"
3"	* 2"	1¾"	126	1¼"
3"	2"	2"	112	1½"
3"	2¼"	2¼"	84	1¾"
4"	2½"	2½"	60	2"
4"	2¾"	3"	50	2½"
4½"	3"	3½"	40	3"
5"	3¾"	4½"	21	4"

Press seams open rather than toward dark fabric.

The illustrations show the strip-pieced fabric shapes that result when strips are stitched for the most common sizes.

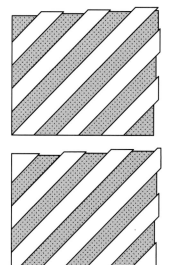
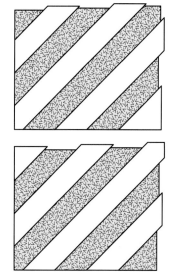

Strip-pieced fabric for 2½" cut (2" finished) bias squares

Strip-pieced fabric for 3½" cut (3" finished) bias squares

Strip-pieced fabric for 4½" cut (4" finished) bias squares

4. Begin cutting at the left side on the lower edge of each unit. Align the 45° mark of the Bias Square ruler on the seam line. Each bias square will require two cuts. The first cut is along the side and top edge. It removes the bias square from the rest of the fabric and is made slightly larger than the correct size. The second cut along the remaining two sides again aligns the diagonal and trims the bias square to the correct size.

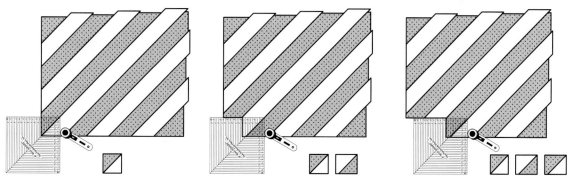

Align 45° mark on seam line and cut first two sides.

5. Turn the cut segments and place the Bias Square on the opposite two sides, accurately aligning the required measurements on both sides of the cutting guide and the 45° mark on the seam. Cut the remaining two sides of the bias squares.

6. Continue cutting bias squares in this manner, working from left to right and from bottom to top, row by row, until you have cut bias squares from all usable fabric. The chart on page 18 specifies how many bias squares you can expect to cut from two fat quarters (18" x 22") of fabric.

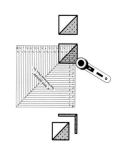

Turn cut segments and cut opposite two sides.

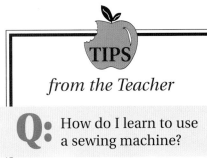
Q: How do I learn to use a sewing machine?

A: It's important to be comfortable with the sewing machine that you are using. If this is your first machine-made quilt, spend a few minutes practicing guiding fabric through the machine. If you leave the machine unthreaded, then you can practice over and over on the same pieces of fabric.

Operating a sewing machine requires the same type of coordination that it takes to drive a car. Use your right foot for the foot pedal to control the speed. If the machine goes too fast at first, slip a sponge under a hinge-type pedal to slow down the speed. Use your hands to guide the fabric that feeds into the machine, similar to the way you steer a car. Sewing requires you to coordinate both hand and foot movements to guide the fabric under the needle.

A good habit to develop is to use a seam ripper or long pin to gently guide the fabric up to the needle. You can hold seam intersections together or make minor adjustments before the fabric is sewn.

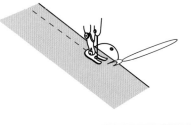

Machine Piecing

The most important skill in machine piecing is sewing an accurate ¼"-wide seam. This is necessary for seams to match and for the resulting block or quilt to measure the required size. There are several methods that will help you achieve this:

1. Purchase a special foot that is sized so that you can align the edge of your fabric with the edge of the presser foot, resulting in a seam that is ¼" away from the fabric edge. Bernina has a special patchwork foot (#37) and Little Foot makes several special ¼" feet that will fit most machines.
2. If you have an electronic or computerized sewing machine, adjust the needle position so that the resulting seam is ¼" away from the fabric edge when using a regular presser foot.
3. Find the ¼" seam allowance on your machine by placing an accurate template under the presser foot and lowering the needle onto the seam line; mark the seam allowance by placing a piece of masking tape at the edge of the template. You can use several layers of masking tape, building up a raised edge to guide your fabric. You can also use a piece of moleskin for a raised seam guide. Test to make sure that the method you are using results in an accurate ¼"-wide seam.

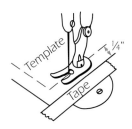

a. Cut three strips of fabric, each 1½" x 3".

b. Sew the strips together, using the edge of the presser foot or the seam guide you have made.

c. Press seams toward the outer edges. After sewing and pressing, the center strip should measure exactly 1" wide. If it doesn't, adjust the needle or seam guide in the proper direction.

Matching Seams

When sewing the fabric pieces that make up a unit or block, follow the piecing diagram provided. Press each group of pieces before joining to the next unit.

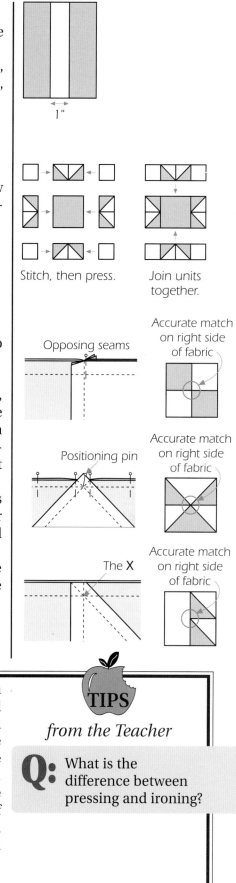

Stitch, then press.   Join units together.

Accurate match on right side of fabric

Opposing seams

Positioning pin

Accurate match on right side of fabric

The X

Accurate match on right side of fabric

There are several techniques that you can use to get your seams to match perfectly.

1. *Opposing Seams:* When stitching one seamed unit to another, press seam allowances on seams that need to match in opposite directions. The two "opposing" seams will hold each other in place and evenly distribute the bulk. Plan pressing to take advantage of opposing seams. You will find this particularly important in strip piecing.

2. *Positioning Pin:* A pin, carefully pushed straight through two points that need to match and pulled tight, will establish the proper point of matching. Pin the remainder of the seam normally and remove the positioning pin just before stitching.

3. *The X:* When triangles are pieced, stitches will form an X at the next seam line. Stitch through the center of the X to make sure the points on the sewn triangles will not be cut off.

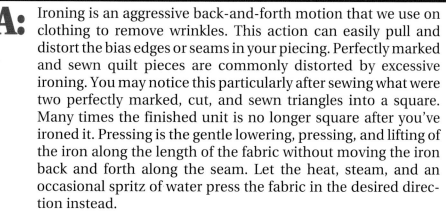

A: Ironing is an aggressive back-and-forth motion that we use on clothing to remove wrinkles. This action can easily pull and distort the bias edges or seams in your piecing. Perfectly marked and sewn quilt pieces are commonly distorted by excessive ironing. You may notice this particularly after sewing what were two perfectly marked, cut, and sewn triangles into a square. Many times the finished unit is no longer square after you've ironed it. Pressing is the gentle lowering, pressing, and lifting of the iron along the length of the fabric without moving the iron back and forth along the seam. Let the heat, steam, and an occasional spritz of water press the fabric in the desired direction instead.

TIPS

from the Teacher

Q: What is the difference between pressing and ironing?

Q: Should I rip out seams that don't match?

A: Inspect each intersection from the right side to see that it is matched. If the seams do not meet accurately, note which direction the fabric needs to be moved. Use a seam ripper to rip out the seam intersection and ½" of stitching on either side of the intersection. Shift fabric to correct alignment, place positioning pins, then restitch.

Shift fabric, place positioning pin, and restitch.

Remove stitching with seam ripper.

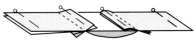

Easing

4. *Easing:* When two pieces you are sewing together are supposed to match but are slightly different in length, pin the points to match and stitch with the shorter piece on top. The feed dog will ease the fullness of the bottom piece.

Chain Piecing

Chain piecing is an assembly-line approach to putting your blocks together. Rather than sewing each block from start to finish, you can sew identical units of each block together at one time, streamlining the process. It's a good idea, however, to sew one sample block together from start to finish to ensure that the pieces have been accurately cut and that you have the proper positioning and coloration for each piece. See Tips from the Teacher on page 24.

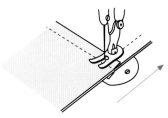

Face top seam allowance toward the needle whenever possible.

Stack the units you will be sewing in pairs, arranging any opposing seam allowances so that the top seam allowance faces toward the needle and the lower seam allowance faces toward you. Then you won't need to keep checking to see if the lower seam is being pulled to the wrong side by the feed dog as you feed the fabric through the sewing machine.

Feed units through the machine without stopping to cut thread. There will be a "stitch" or small length of thread between units that needs to be clipped.

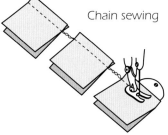

Chain sewing

Take connected units to the ironing board for pressing, then clip apart. Chain piecing takes a little planning, but it will save you time and thread.

A: Use a thread saver to begin and end all your seams. Keep a stack of fabric scraps, about 2" x 2", near your machine. When you begin to sew, fold one of the squares in half and sew to its edge. Leave the presser foot down and continue sewing onto your piecing unit. When you have finished sewing a seam or chain piecing, sew onto another thread saver and leave the needle in place and the presser foot down. This thread saver will be in place for sewing the next seam or unit.

Q: How can I save thread and keep the back of my patch-work neat?

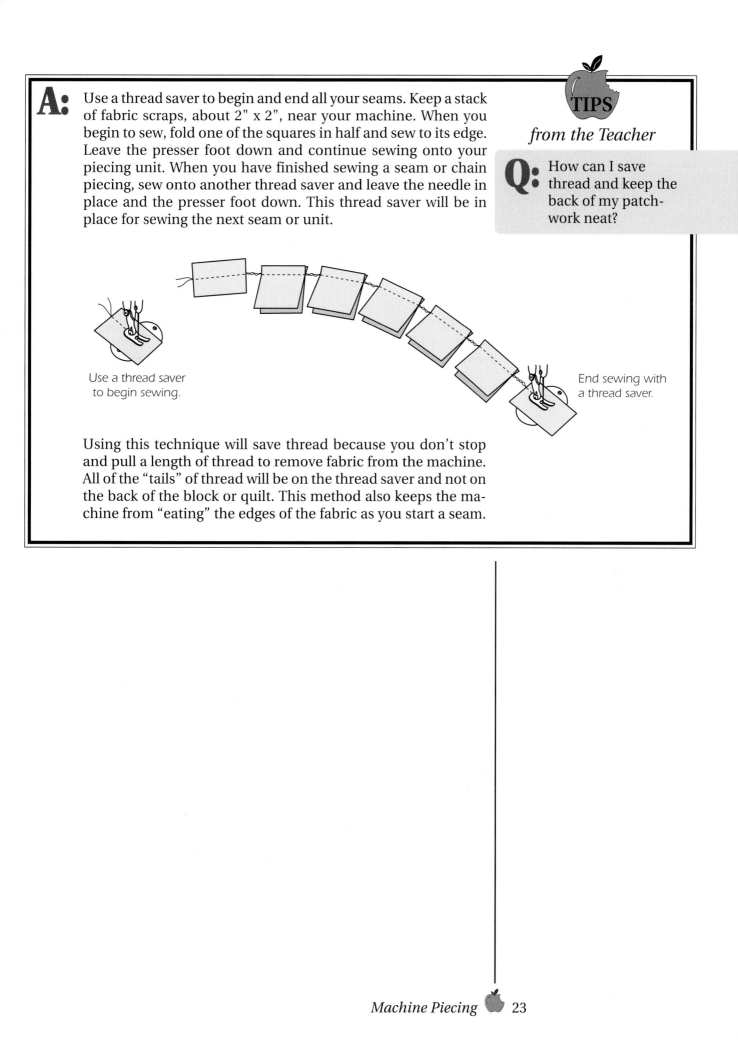

Use a thread saver to begin sewing.

End sewing with a thread saver.

Using this technique will save thread because you don't stop and pull a length of thread to remove fabric from the machine. All of the "tails" of thread will be on the thread saver and not on the back of the block or quilt. This method also keeps the machine from "eating" the edges of the fabric as you start a seam.

Using This Book

Complete instructions are provided for ten rotary-cut quilts in a variety of sizes. All of the patterns are written for rotary cutting; no templates are provided. Study the color photos carefully and read the complete cutting and piecing directions for the quilt you are going to make before you begin. It's also a good idea to make a sample block. See Tips from the Teacher below.

Fabric requirements are based on fat quarters (18" x 22" pieces of fabric) and 44"-wide fabric that has 42 usable inches after preshrinking. If your fabric is smaller than these sizes, you may need to purchase more. The amounts given are adequate for the project; there will be little leftover fabric.

Cutting instructions are presented in easy-to-read charts. Quick-cutting and strip-piecing techniques sometimes yield more pieces than are actually needed to make a particular block or quilt; don't worry if you have a few more pieces than you need. All measurements for block pieces include ¼"-wide seam allowances. *Do not add seam allowances to the dimesions given in the cutting section.*

Cutting specifications for triangles indicate the size of the square from which you cut the triangles. Directions for half-square triangles use this symbol ◻; quarter-square triangles use this symbol ⊠. If you need a refresher, see pages 12–13.

Quick-cutting methods vary from pattern to pattern; in each case, I have selected the technique most appropriate to the particular quilt. All of the methods used are thoroughly explained in the section on Rotary Cutting.

Use the photos and drawings that accompany the patterns as a reference while assembling your quilt. All borders have straight-cut corners rather than mitered corners. Border strips are cut along the crosswise grain and seamed where extra length is needed; purchase additional fabric if you want to cut borders along the lengthwise grain. Border pieces are cut extra long, then trimmed to fit when the actual dimensions of the quilt top are known. See pages 77–78.

General instructions for finishing your quilt begin on page 77.

TIPS

from the Teacher

Q: What is a sample block?

A: A sample block is a test block that you stitch together before making your quilt to ensure that the quilt will be to your liking. Check to see that all pieces have been cut correctly and match accurately. You may also want to evaluate the color placement. If you are satisfied with the block and the cutting, then you are ready to chain-piece or speed-piece your quilt top.

Gallery

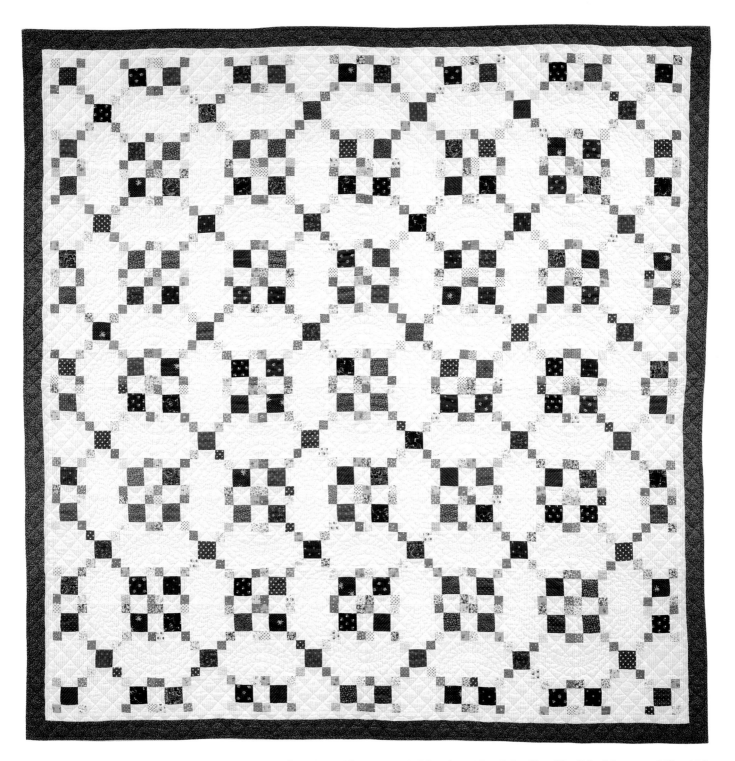

Puss in the Corner by Nancy J. Martin, 1985, Woodinville, Washington, 80" x 80".
A varied collection of blue fabrics with both light and dark backgrounds is set against a solid
white fabric, highlighting the elaborate hand quilting by Judy Eide. Directions on page 46.

A Little Bit of Irish Luck by Cleo Nollette, 1993, Seattle, Washington, 44" x 44". This Irish Chain–type quilt features a lovely background print, accented with a seasoned collection of blue fabrics. A perfect choice for a beginner, this quilt is enhanced by a machine-quilted grid pattern. Directions on page 38.

Quilt Backs: Straight and Narrow, left; Antique Ocean Waves, center; and Bright Lights, right. Construct a few extra blocks or use leftover components from the front of the quilt to piece a backing. See Tips from the Teacher on page 80.

*Stars and Stripes Forever by Nancy J. Martin, 1993, Woodinville, Washington, 42" x 56".
Patriotic fabrics in red and blue feature star, flag, and Columbus Day motifs. The tan patriotic
fabrics create the background for the "chain" that results when these Puss in the Corner blocks
are combined. Quilted by Sue von Jentzen. Directions on page 46.*

Delectable Mountains by Nancy J. Martin, 1987, Woodinville, Washington, 68" x 68". This angular red-and-white design is softened by the feather quilting in the center wreath and inner border. Quilted by Beverly Payne. Directions on page 65.

Purple Mountain Majesty by Cleo Nollette, 1993, Seattle, Washington, 48" x 48". A scrappy version of Delectable Mountains is created by using an assortment of purple fabrics. The consistent background print helps to unify the design. Quilted by Nancy Sweeney. Directions on page 65.

Liberty on the Loose by Nancy J. Martin, 1993, Woodinville, Washington, 45" x 45". Liberty of London™ fabrics, collected while on a teaching trip to Australia, are combined in this mock Log Cabin design. Quilted by Nancy Sweeney. Directions on page 62.

Go to a Neutral Corner by Nancy J. Martin, 1993, Woodinville, Washington, 85" x 85". Beige is considered to be a neutral color by many quilters, but contrasting light and dark beige backgrounds produce a quiet, restful overtone to this angular mock Log Cabin design. The circular quilting design executed by Sue von Jentzen continues into the border and further softens the design. Directions on page 62.

Straight and Narrow by Nancy J. Martin, 1983, Woodinville, Washington, 72" x 72". An Amish-inspired color scheme, using muted solid-colored fabrics, is found in this Straight Furrows design. The black quilting thread is especially evident on the elaborate rose border design. Anonymous quilter. Directions on page 55.

Tapestry by Cleo Nollette, 1993, Seattle, Washington, 44" x 52". The rich paisley fabric used in the border defines the color scheme for this strip-pieced Straight Furrows quilt. Directions on page 55.

Bright Lights by Cleo Nollette, 1993, Seattle, Washington, 42" x 54". Bright colors sparkling across several light background prints are sure to delight baby's eyes. The machine quilting by Roxanne Carter and scrappy binding add the perfect finishing touches. Directions on page 42.

Vintage Barn Raising by Dan and Nancy J. Martin, 1993, Woodinville, Washington, 66" x 66". Reproduction fabrics, reminiscent of those used in the 1870s–1890s, rest against a variety of double-pink prints to create an antique look. There is even a "religious error" created by the turning of a block. Can you find it? Quilted by Donna Gundlach. Directions on page 42.

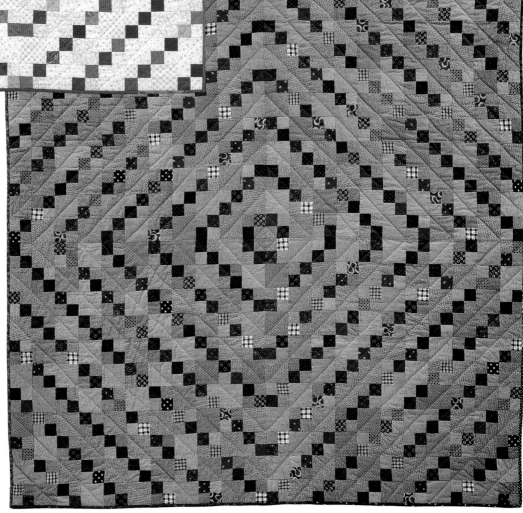

*Good Things Come in Small Packages by Cleo Nollette, 1993, Seattle, Washington, 48" x 56".
This delicate pastel color scheme used for the Envelope blocks makes a perfect baby quilt that
would enhance any nursery. Machine quilted by Roxanne Carter. Directions on page 59.*

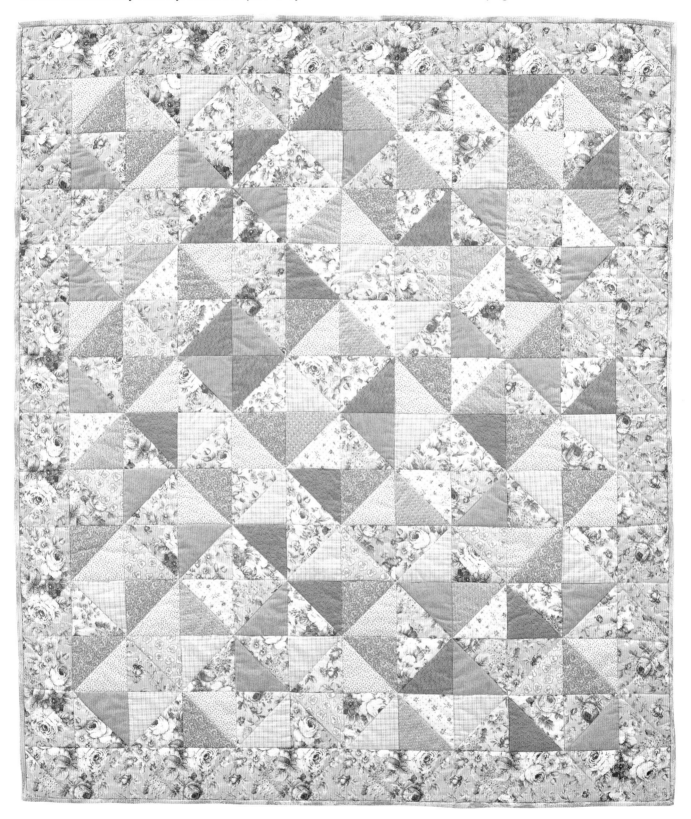

*Foreign Mail by Nancy J. Martin, 1993, Woodinville, Washington, 80" x 96". Reproduction
and authentic antique chintzes collected while on a visit to the Netherlands are combined
in this Envelope quilt. Quilted by Beverly Payne. Directions on page 59.*

Indian Trails, maker unknown, c. 1930, North Carolina, 92" x 104".
The green print used for the alternate blocks provides a welcome
complement to the classic red, white, and blue color scheme.
Collection of Nancy J. Martin. Directions on page 70.

Red Snails in the Sunset by Cleo Nollette, 1992, Seattle, Washington, 76" x 76". Assorted red prints set against a swirling red-and-white background liven this classic Snail's Trail quilt. This challenging variation requires careful planning to match the red prints. Quilted by Teresa Haskins. Directions for a scrappy Snail's Trail on page 73.

Ancient Snails by Nancy J. Martin, 1993, Woodinville, Washington, 38½" x 45½". A scrappy quilt made from contrasting light and dark fabrics will create visual excitement when hung on a wall. Directions on page 73.

Pinwheel Squares by Nancy J. Martin, 1993, Woodinville, Washington, 60" x 90". This design was inspired by an antique quilt seen in Nebraska. Speed-piecing techniques allow you to construct this modern-day version in a fraction of the time needed to make the original. Directions on page 50.

Pretty in Pink by Nancy J. Martin, 1993, Woodinville, Washington, 45" x 60". Reproduction fabrics similar to those used in the 1930s make up this charming quilt. This is a good project to utilize coordinated packages of fat quarters. Directions on page 50.

A: It's helpful to know the names of the parts of a quilt. Study the diagram below and the labels that point to various quilt parts.

Q: Are there any special quilt terms that I should know?

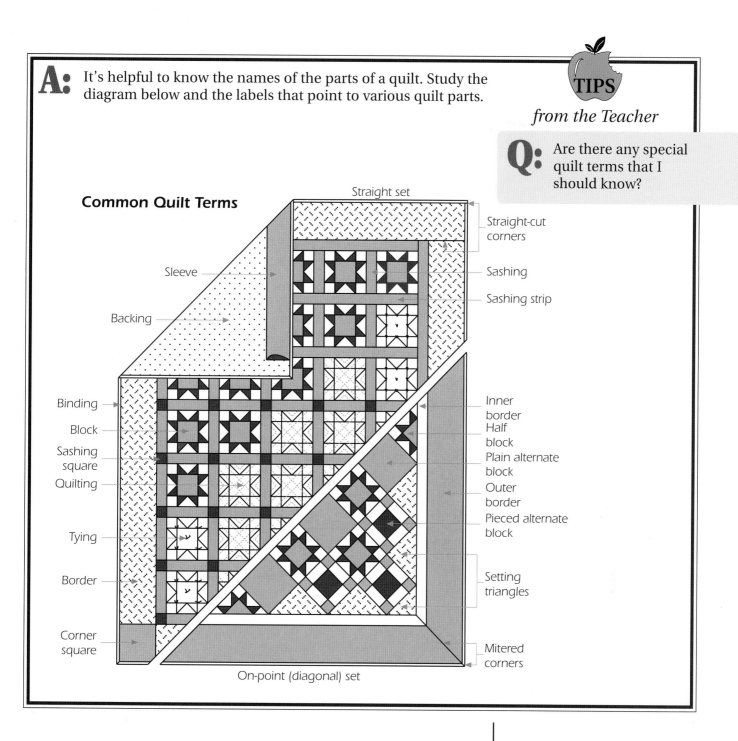

Common Quilt Terms

Straight set

Straight-cut corners

Sashing

Sashing strip

Sleeve

Backing

Binding

Block

Sashing square

Quilting

Tying

Border

Corner square

Inner border

Half block

Plain alternate block

Outer border

Pieced alternate block

Setting triangles

Mitered corners

On-point (diagonal) set

Ninepatch

4½" Block

This pattern is a good choice for your first quilt. You'll practice an easy strip-piecing method for this traditional block. When these blocks are sewn together, a "chain" appears across the quilt top. Color photo on page 26.

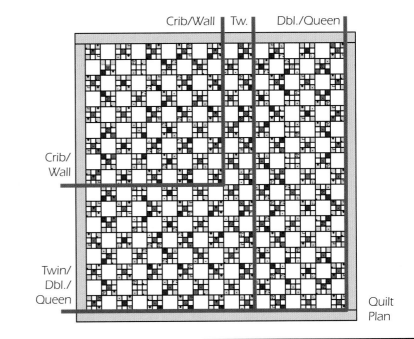

Crib/Wall Tw. Dbl./Queen

Crib/
Wall

Twin/
Dbl./
Queen

Quilt
Plan

	Crib/Wall	Twin	Dbl/Q
Finished Size	48½" x 48½"	57½" x 84½"	84½" x 84½"
Ninepatch Blocks	41	94	145
Alternate Blocks	40	93	144
Block Layout	9 x 9	11 x 17	17 x 17
Border Width	4"	4"	4"

Materials: *44"-wide fabric*

	Crib/Wall	Twin	Dbl/Q
Light Fabric	6 fat qtrs.	13 fat qtrs.	19 fat qtrs.
Dark Fabric	4 fat qtrs.	7 fat qtrs.	10 fat qtrs.
Border	¾ yd.	1 yd.	1⅛ yds.
Binding	½ yd.	⅝ yd.	⅝ yd.
Backing	2¾ yds.	3¼ yds.	4½ yds.

Cutting

Fabric	Strip Length	Strip Width	Number of Strips		
			Crib/Wall	Twin	Dbl/Q
Light	21"	2"	20	40	60
	21"	5"	10	24	36
Dark	21"	2"	25	50	75
Border	42"	4¼"	5	7	9

Directions

NINEPATCH BLOCKS

1. Stitch 2"-wide light and dark strips together as shown to make Strip Set 1. Press seams toward darker fabric.

Strip Set 1

Strip size before sewing — 2" 2" 2"

Make 10 sets (crib).
20 sets (twin).
30 sets (dbl./queen).

2. Stitch 2"-wide light and dark strips together as shown to make Strip Set 2. Press seams toward darker fabric.

Strip Set 2

Strip size before sewing — 2" 2" 2"

Make 5 sets (crib).
10 sets (twin).
15 sets (dbl./queen).

3. Place a Strip Set 1 and a Strip Set 2 together with right sides facing as shown at right.
4. Cut the strip sets into pairs of 2" units, beginning at the left side of the strips and working toward the right.
5. Stitch pairs together with ¼"-wide seams. See page 22 for chain piecing.

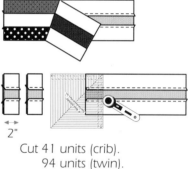

Cut 41 units (crib).
94 units (twin).
145 units (dbl./queen).

6. Cut 2" units from remaining sets of Strip Set 1. Cut 41 units for crib, 94 units for twin, and 145 units for double/queen.
7. Stitch remaining 2" units to previously sewn pairs of 2" units to make Ninepatch blocks.
8. Press seams as shown.

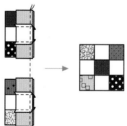

Pressing guide

ALTERNATE BLOCKS

From 5"-wide strips of light fabric, cut:
   40 squares, each 5" x 5", for the crib
   93 squares, each 5" x 5", for the twin
   144 squares, each 5" x 5", for the double/queen

Quilt Top Assembly and Finishing

1. Arrange Ninepatch and 5" alternate blocks as shown in the quilt plan on page 38. Make sure the top and bottom rows have a Ninepatch on each end. Sew blocks in horizontal rows. Press

seams in opposite directions from row to row. Join rows together, making sure to match the seams between the blocks.

2. To add borders, seam 4¼" border strips as necessary. Measure and stitch borders to sides, then to top and bottom edges of quilt top. See pages 77–78.
3. Layer quilt top with batting and backing; baste.
4. Quilt as desired or tie.
5. Bind with bias strips of fabric.

QUILTING SUGGESTION

TIPS

from the Teacher

Q: How do I choose fabrics for a scrappy quilt?

A: First look to see if your quilt has a "background" on which a pattern will appear. Most quilts do. If so, select your background fabric first. Don't limit your choices to solid colors, even though muslin is a traditional background fabric for scrap quilts. If you really want to use a solid-colored fabric, try a deep turkey red or perhaps black or navy for an Amish look. Remember solid-colored fabrics tend to emphasize mismatched seams and irregular quilting stitches. If you are a beginner who is still perfecting your piecing and quilting skills, select a print that is more likely to hide minor imperfections.

Choose a background print that is nondirectional and still appears unified after being cut apart and resewn. Study the examples below for good and poor choices of background fabric.

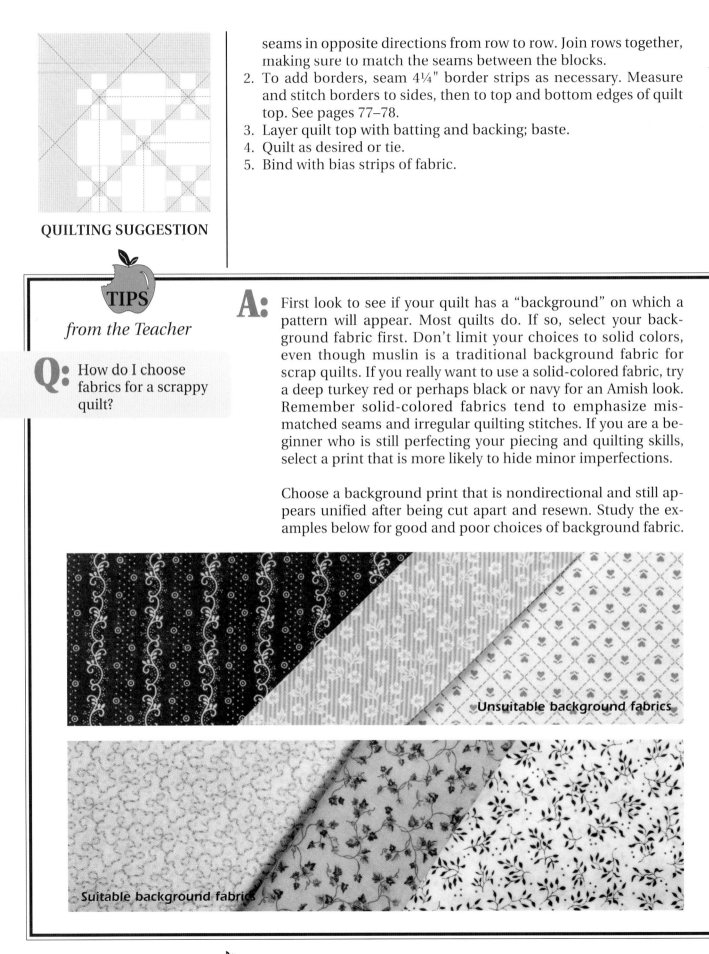

Unsuitable background fabrics

Suitable background fabrics

To test the suitability of background fabrics while shopping, make several directional folds and evaluate the unity of the design.

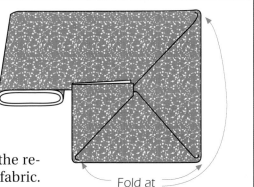

Fold at right angles.

Prints with a white background have a clean, formal look; those with a beige or tan background resemble antique quilts and have a more informal look.

Once you have chosen the "background fabric," select the remaining fabrics which will enhance the background fabric. Study the colors that appear in the design on the background fabric and begin your selection. If working with a single color family, such as blue, select a wide range of blue fabrics. Begin with deep, dark navy blue, adding royal blue, medium blues, and then light blues. If most of your blue fabrics are bright, then stick to bright blues in all shades. If your blue fabrics are dull or "grayed," then select muted shades of blue fabrics. Study the photo of A Little Bit of Irish Luck on page 26 to see the wide range of blue fabrics selected.

Because you will be working with scraps or fat quarters, you may be using a number of different fabrics to represent a single value. When cutting the pieces shown as dark in the quilt plan, for example, you can use two, three, or ten different dark fabrics. These might be all the same color (like an assortment of reds) or different colors of the same value (like a combination of dark blues, dark greens, and browns).

As you grow more experienced in selecting fabrics, you may also want to select a wide range of fabrics to use as the background rather than a single fabric. Study the photo of the Vintage Barn Raising on page 31. Note the wide range of pink prints used as the background.

Double Four Patch

6" Block

Joining Block

Center Block

This quick and easy quilt uses Four Patch blocks created from strip piecing and arranged in a Barn Raising setting. This is a good quilt to use those extra strips for the rows of squares, and fat quarters for the background fabric. Color photos on page 31.

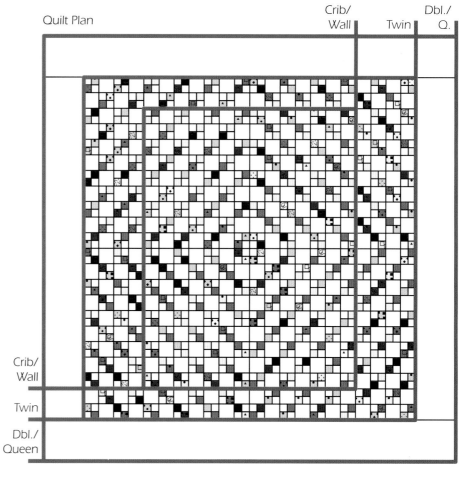

Quilt Plan

Crib/Wall

Twin

Dbl./Q.

Crib/Wall

Twin

Dbl./Queen

	Crib/Wall	Twin	Dbl/Q*
Finished Size	42" x 54"	66" x 66"	82" x 82"
Blocks	63	121	121
Block Layout	7 x 9	11 x 11	11 x 11

The Dbl/Q size includes an 8" border.

Materials: *44"-wide fabric*

	Crib/Wall	Twin	Dbl/Q
Light Fabric	9 fat qtrs.	17 fat qtrs.	17 fat qtrs.
Dark Fabric*	6 fat qtrs.	9 fat qtrs.	10 fat qtrs.
Border	—	—	2 yds.
Binding**	½ yd.	⅝ yd.	¾ yd.
Backing	1½ yds.	4 yds.	4⅞ yds.

Piece extra dark fabric to make straight-grain multicolor binding. See pages 84–86 .
**Yardage required for binding from single fabric.*

Cutting

Fabric	Strip Length	Strip Width	Crib/Wall	Twin	Dbl/Q
Light	21"	2"	28	50	50
	21"	3½"	25	48	48
Dark	21"	2"	28	50	50
Border	42"	8¼"	—	—	8

Number of Strips spans the Crib/Wall, Twin, and Dbl/Q columns.

Directions

DOUBLE FOUR PATCH BLOCKS

1. From 3½"-wide assorted light strips, cut:
   124 squares, each 3½" x 3½", for crib/wall size
   240 squares, each 3½" x 3½", for twin and double/queen size
2. Sew 2"-wide light and dark strips together randomly to make different strip sets. Press seams toward the darker fabric.
3. Layer 2 strip sets together with right sides facing as shown.
4. Cut strip sets into 2" units, leaving units stacked after cutting.

Make 28 sets (crib).
50 sets (twin/dbl./queen).

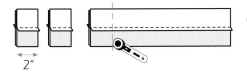

2"

Cut 128 units (crib).
244 units (twin/dbl./queen).

5. Carefully pick up units and stitch together to make Four Patch units. See page 22 for chain-piecing details.

Make 128 (crib).
244 (twin/dbl./queen).

6. Join 2 Four Patch units and two 3½" squares as shown to make a Double Four Patch block.

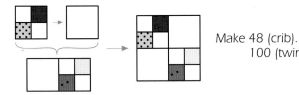

Make 48 (crib).
100 (twin/dbl./queen).

CENTER BLOCK

Join 4 Four Patch units as shown to make the center block.

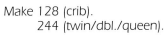

Make 1.

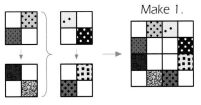

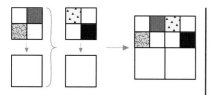

Make 14 (crib).
20 (twin/dbl./queen).

JOINING BLOCKS

Join remaining Four Patch units and 3½" x 3½" squares as shown to make joining blocks.

Quilt Top Assembly and Finishing

1. Join the blocks as shown below.

   NOTE: Illustrations are for crib size; add necessary blocks for larger size.

   a. Arrange the Double Four Patch blocks as shown to make 1 quarter section. Sew blocks in horizontal rows. Press seams in opposite directions from row to row. Join rows together, making sure to match the seams between the blocks. Repeat to make 3 more quarter sections.

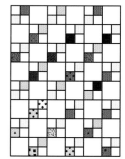

   Make 4 quarter sections.

   b. Stitch the joining blocks together as shown to make 2 vertical rows and 2 horizontal rows.

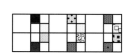

Make 2 horizontal rows.

Make 2 vertical rows.

   c. Sew the vertical rows between 2 quarter sections. Be sure to rotate the quarter sections as shown.

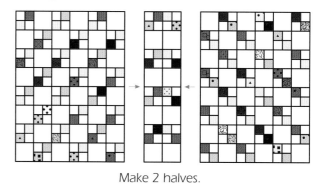

   Make 2 halves.

   d. Sew the center block between the 2 horizontal rows.

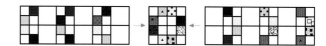

e. Join the 2 halves and the horizontal row as shown.

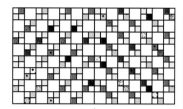

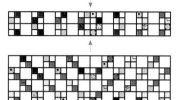

2. For the double/queen size quilt, add 8¼" borders, seaming strips as necessary. Measure and stitch borders to the sides, then to the top and bottom edges of the quilt top. See pages 77–78.
3. Layer quilt top with batting and backing; baste.
4. Quilt as desired or tie.
5. Bind with bias strips of fabric.

QUILTING SUGGESTION

A: Binding can be made from strips cut on the straight grain or on the bias grain.

To make straight-grain binding:

Remove a 2¼"-wide strip from each dark fat quarter used in the quilt top before cutting strips for quilt blocks. Use the Bias Square to cut both ends of each strip at a 45° angle.

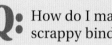

Cut both ends at a 45° angle.

Join strips together, using a ¼"-wide seam allowance and off-setting angled ends as shown.

To make bias-grain binding:

If you made a quilt with bias squares, save several of the bias strips to make a scrappy binding. It will not be necessary to angle the ends of the strips, since they will already have angled ends.

Cut and piece together binding strips to make enough binding to go around the perimeter of the quilt, plus 5" or 6". There is no need to purchase additional yardage for this type of binding. Yardage requirements given in the Materials chart for light and dark fabrics are adequate for quilt blocks and scrappy binding. If you want to make the binding from a single fabric, yardage for binding is provided in the Materials chart.

Bind quilt after quilting is complete, using either straight-cut or bias strips and following the directions on pages 84–86.

TIPS
from the Teacher

Q: How do I make a scrappy binding?

Puss in the Corner

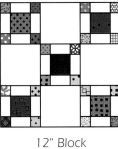

12" Block

This traditional pattern is ideal for using scraps or packets of fat quarters. Select a single background fabric or purchase fat quarters to vary the background prints. Color photos on pages 25 and 27.

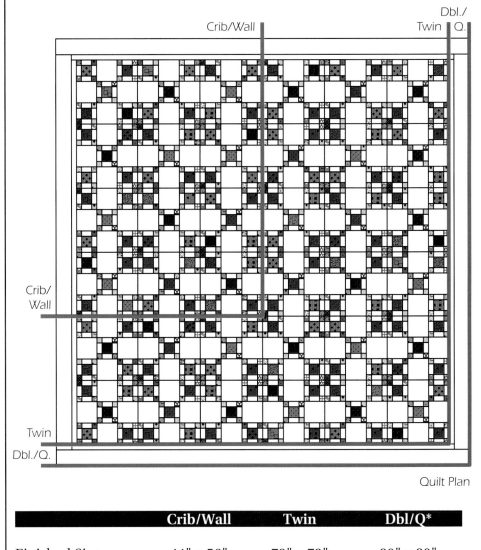

Quilt Plan

	Crib/Wall	Twin	Dbl/Q*
Finished Size	44" x 56"	72" x 72"	80" x 80"
No. of Blocks	12	36	36
Block Layout	3 x 4	6 x 6	6 x 6
Border Width	4"	—	1" inner; 3" outer

Materials: 44"-wide fabric

	Crib/Wall	Twin	Dbl/Q*
Light Fabric	7 fat qtrs.	19 fat qtrs.	19 fat qtrs.
Dark Fabric	4 fat qtrs.	9 fat qtrs.	9 fat qtrs.
Inner Border	—	—	½ yd.
Outer Border	¾ yd.	—	⅞ yd.
Binding	½ yd.	⅝ yd.	¾ yd.
Backing	1¾ yds.	4⅛ yds.	4⅝ yds.

Fabric	Strip Length	Strip Width	Number of Strips Crib/Wall	Twin	Dbl/Q
Light	21"	1½"	16	46	46
	21"	2½"	10	28	28
	21"	4½"	12	36	36
Dark	21"	1½"	20	56	56
	21"	2½"	8	23	23
Inner Border	42"	1½"	—	—	7
Outer Border	42"	3¼"	—	—	8
Outer Border	42"	4¼"	5	—	—

Directions

PUSS IN THE CORNER UNITS

1. Stitch strips together as shown to make Strip Set 1. Press seams toward darker fabric. Cut Strip Set 1 into 2½"-wide units.

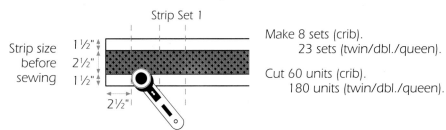

Strip size before sewing
1½"
2½"
1½"
2½"

Make 8 sets (crib).
   23 sets (twin/dbl./queen).

Cut 60 units (crib).
   180 units (twin/dbl./queen).

2. Stitch strips together as shown to make Strip Set 2. Press seams toward darker fabric. Cut Strip Set 2 into 1½"-wide units.

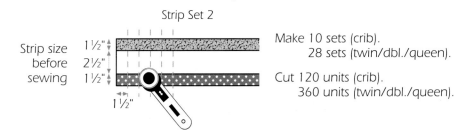

Strip size before sewing
1½"
2½"
1½"
1½"

Make 10 sets (crib).
   28 sets (twin/dbl./queen).

Cut 120 units (crib).
   360 units (twin/dbl./queen).

3. Stitch a unit from Strip Set 1 between 2 units from Strip Set 2 as shown to make a Puss in the Corner unit.
4. From the 4½"-wide strips of light fabric, cut:
   48 squares, each 4½" x 4½", for the crib size
   144 squares, each 4½" x 4½", for the twin size
   144 squares, each 4½" x 4½", for the double/queen size

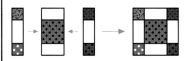

Make 60 (crib).
   180 (twin/dbl./queen).

Quilt Top Assembly and Finishing

1. Assemble 5 Puss in the Corner units and four 4½" squares as shown to make a Puss in the Corner block.

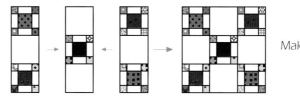

Make 12 (crib).
36 (twin/dbl./queen).

2. Arrange blocks as shown in the quilt plan on page 46. Sew blocks in horizontal rows. Press seams in opposite directions from row to row. Join rows, making sure to match the seams between the blocks.

3. *For crib size:* Add borders, seaming 4¼"-wide border strips as necessary. Measure and stitch borders to sides, then to top and bottom edges of quilt top. See pages 77–78.

   For double/queen size: Add inner border, seaming 1½"-wide border strips as necessary. Measure and stitch borders to sides, then to top and bottom edges of quilt top. See pages 77–78. Repeat with 3¼"-wide outer border strips.

4. Layer quilt top with batting and backing; baste.
5. Quilt as desired or tie.
6. Bind with bias strips of fabric.

QUILTING SUGGESTION

Use a heart and feather design that forms an arc around the center section. For faster quilting or machine quilting, stitch a diagonal grid in both directions through the blocks.

A: If the quilt is a scrappy quilt that uses fabric randomly, don't worry about the placement of stripes or plaids. Let them fall as they are cut, including off-grain plaids with stripes going both horizontally and vertically.

from the Teacher

Q: How do I use directional fabrics in a quilt?

Controlling the direction of striped fabric requires careful cutting and placement. For example, in cutting half-square triangles, cut half the triangles in one direction and the remaining triangles in the opposite direction.

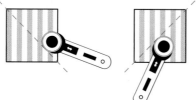

When sewing striped fabric to a square or diamond, place the stripes from squares cut in one direction to opposite sides of the square.

Then sew the stripes from squares cut in the opposite direction to the remaining sides of the square.

To center a design from a pictorial or theme print, use a see-through ruler and adjust the crosswise cuts to center the design.

Pinwheel Square

15" Block

Packs of fat quarters are ideal for this strip-pieced quilt. Reproduction 1930s fabrics were used in the crib size, while reproduction 1890s prints were used in the twin size. Color photos on page 36.

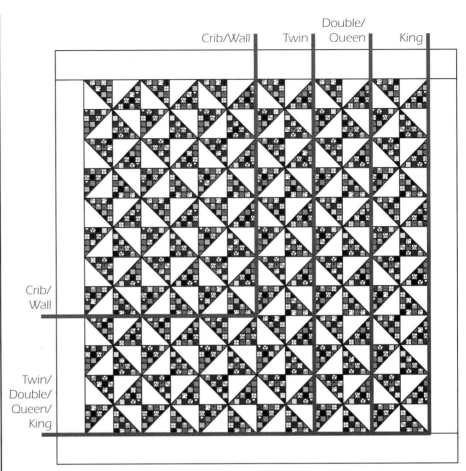

Crib/Wall

Double/Queen

Twin

King

Crib/Wall

Twin/Double/Queen/King

Quilt Plan

	Crib/Wall	Twin	Dbl/Q	King
Finished Size	45" x 60"	60" x 90"	91" x 106"	106" x 106"
No. of Blocks	12	24	30	36
Block Layout	3 x 4	4 x 6	5 x 6	6 x 6
Border Width	—	—	8"	8"

Materials: *44"-wide fabric*

	Crib/Wall	Twin	Dbl/Q	King
Light Fabric	5 fat qtrs.	9 fat qtrs.	11 fat qtrs.	12 fat qtrs.
Dark Fabric	7 fat qtrs.	13 fat qtrs.	16 fat qtrs.	18 fat qtrs.
Accent Fabric	1¼ yds.	2½ yds.	5½ yds.*	6½ yds.*
Binding	½ yd.	⅝ yd.	¾ yd.	⅞ yd.
Backing	2¾ yds.	3½ yds.	6 yds.	9 yds.

Includes yardage for borders.

Cutting

Fabric	Strip Length	Strip Width	Number of Strips			
			Crib/Wall	Twin	Dbl/Q	King
Light	21"	2"	36	66	84	96
Dark	21"	2"	54	99	126	144

From accent and border fabric, cut borders from the lengthwise grain of the fabric for double/queen and king first. The crib and twin do not have borders.

For double/queen size, cut 4 strips, each 8¼" x 92"
For king size, cut 2 strips, each 8¼" x 92" and 2 strips, each 8¼" x 107"

From accent fabric (remainder of accent fabric for queen and king), cut 8⅜" x 8⅜" squares, then cut once diagonally to yield half-square triangles. See chart below for the number of squares and triangles to cut for the size quilt you are making.

	Crib/Wall	Twin	Dbl/Q	King
No. of Squares	24	48	60	72
◻ No. of Triangles	48	96	120	144

Directions

PINWHEEL BLOCK

1. Stitch strips together to make strip sets as shown at right. See chart below for number of strip sets to make and the number of 2" units to cut from each strip set for the size quilt you are making. Cut remaining 2" dark strips into 2" squares.

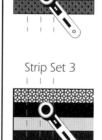

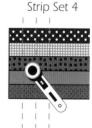

Strip Set 1   Strip Set 2

Strip Set 3   Strip Set 4

	Crib/Wall		Twin		Dbl/Q		King	
	No. Sets	2" Units	No. Sets	2" Units	No. Sets	2" Units	No. Sets	2" Units
Strip Set 1	6	48	11	96	14	120	16	144
Strip Set 2	6	48	11	96	14	120	16	144
Strip Set 3	6	48	11	96	14	120	16	144
Strip Set 4	6	48	11	96	14	120	16	144
2" Dark Strip	6	48	11	96	14	120	16	144

2. Assemble one 2" unit from each strip set and a 2" dark square to make a stair-step unit as shown. Press seams in one direction.

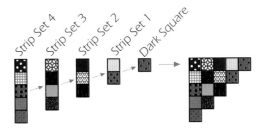

3. Working from the wrong side of the stair-step unit, place the ¼" mark of a ruler over the seam intersections as shown. Trim to create a triangle.

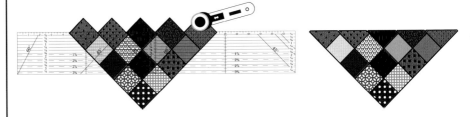

4. Sew a trimmed triangle unit to a half-square triangle cut from the accent fabric as shown, to make one quarter of a Pinwheel block.
5. Join 4 quarter sections as shown to make a Pinwheel block.

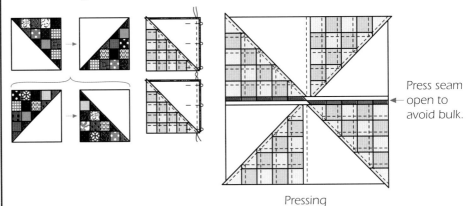

Press seam open to avoid bulk.

Pressing

Quilt Top Assembly and Finishing

1. Arrange blocks as shown in the quilt plan on page 50. Sew blocks into horizontal rows. Press seams in opposite directions from row to row. Join rows, making sure to match the seams between the blocks.
2. Add borders for double/queen and king size. Measure and stitch borders to sides, then to the top and bottom edges of the quilt top. See page 77–78.
3. Layer quilt top with batting and backing; baste.
4. Quilt as desired or tie.
5. Bind with bias strips of fabric.

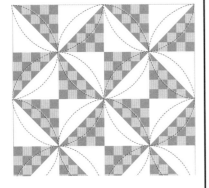

QUILTING SUGGESTION

A: For each quilt block to contain a variety of fabrics, you must vary the strips in the strip sets. Select a different combination of fabric for each strip set and vary the position of the fabric within the strip sets. Study the different fabric combinations for Strip Sets 3 and 4 of the Pinwheel Square quilt.

Q: How can I avoid having identical fabric combinations when I strip-piece?

Strip Set 3

Strip Set 4

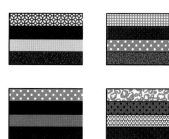

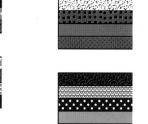

The completed blocks will have varied fabric combinations.

A: Many designs, such as Straight Furrows (page 55), have repetitions of the same fabric but in slightly different positions. The fabrics are repeated in a diagonal pattern by moving one square either up or down from row to row.

Q: How can I adapt strip-piecing to repeating designs?

You can utilize strip-piecing in these designs by sewing together strips of fabric. Each strip of fabric is given a number and sewn in a specified order. The strips are then cut into units of a certain size. Before resewing the strips together, the unit is broken apart at a specified point by pulling out the stitching. This unit is then resewn after moving the divided portion into a different position. Sometimes certain squares are discarded before resewing.

The grid shown at right is a simplified example of how fabrics are repeated using finished 2" squares. Study the number grid for the design. Each column of fabric has a letter name.

A	B	C	D	E
5	4	3	2	1
4	3	2	1	5
3	2	1	5	4
2	1	5	4	3
1	5	4	3	2

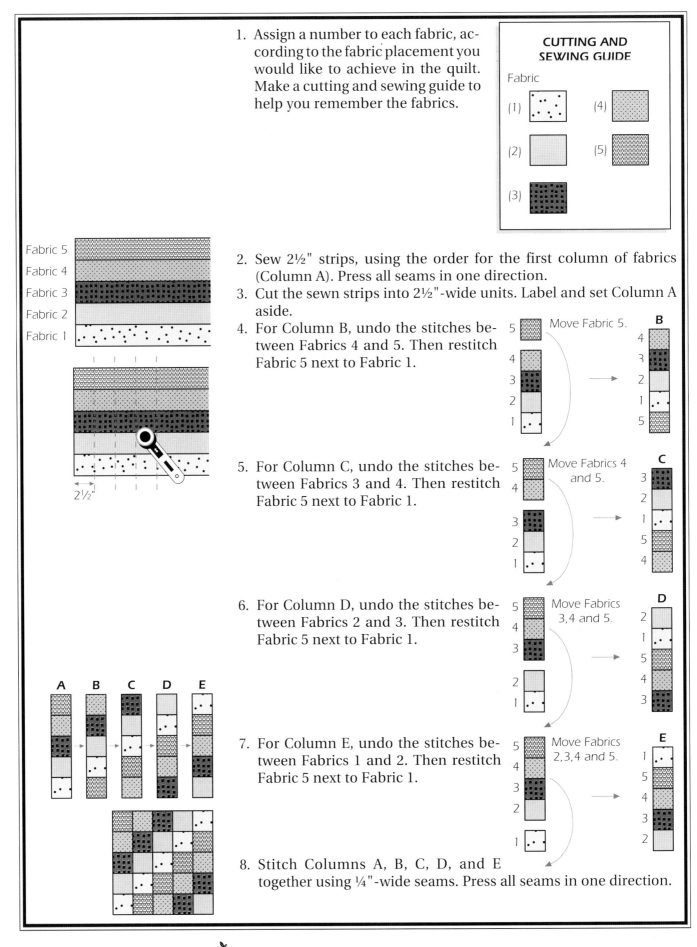

CUTTING AND
SEWING GUIDE

Fabric

(1)   (4)

(2)   (5)

(3)

1. Assign a number to each fabric, according to the fabric placement you would like to achieve in the quilt. Make a cutting and sewing guide to help you remember the fabrics.

Fabric 5
Fabric 4
Fabric 3
Fabric 2
Fabric 1

2½"

2. Sew 2½" strips, using the order for the first column of fabrics (Column A). Press all seams in one direction.

3. Cut the sewn strips into 2½"-wide units. Label and set Column A aside.

4. For Column B, undo the stitches between Fabrics 4 and 5. Then restitch Fabric 5 next to Fabric 1.

Move Fabric 5.

B
4
3
2
1
5

5. For Column C, undo the stitches between Fabrics 3 and 4. Then restitch Fabric 5 next to Fabric 1.

Move Fabrics 4 and 5.

C
3
2
1
5
4

6. For Column D, undo the stitches between Fabrics 2 and 3. Then restitch Fabric 5 next to Fabric 1.

Move Fabrics 3, 4 and 5.

D
2
1
5
4
3

7. For Column E, undo the stitches between Fabrics 1 and 2. Then restitch Fabric 5 next to Fabric 1.

Move Fabrics 2, 3, 4 and 5.

E
1
5
4
3
2

8. Stitch Columns A, B, C, D, and E together using ¼"-wide seams. Press all seams in one direction.

A   B   C   D   E

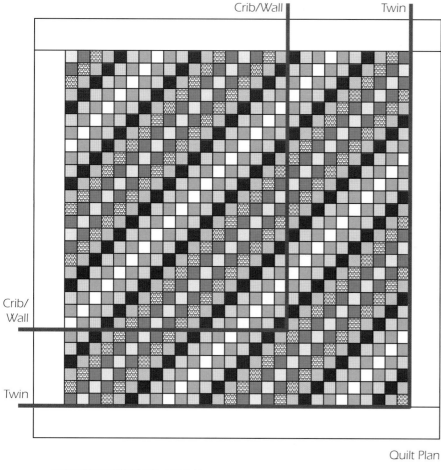

Crib/Wall   Twin

Crib/
Wall

Twin

Quilt Plan

Straight Furrows

This strip-pieced quilt uses eight different fabrics and can be quickly cut and sewn. Practice the technique shown on pages 53–54 before doing the wall hanging or twin size. Color photos on page 30.

	Crib/Wall	Twin
Finished Size	44" x 52"	72" x 72"

Materials: *44"-wide fabric*

	Crib/Wall	Twin
Fabric 1	1 fat qtr.	1 fat qtr.
Fabric 2	1 fat qtr.	2 fat qtrs.
Fabric 3	1 fat qtr.	2 fat qtrs.
Fabric 4	1 fat qtr.	2 fat qtrs.
Fabric 5	1 fat qtr.	2 fat qtrs.
Fabric 6	1 fat qtr.	2 fat qtrs.
Fabric 7	1 fat qtr.	2 fat qtrs.
Fabric 8	1 fat qtr.	1 fat qtr.
Border	¾ yd.	2⅛ yds.
Binding	⅜ yd.	⅝ yd.
Backing	1⅝ yds.	4¼ yds.

Cutting

Fabric	Strip Length	Strip Width	Number of Strips Crib/Wall	Twin
Fabric 1	21"	2"	2	6
Fabric 2	21"	2"	4	12
Fabric 3	21"	2"	6	12
Fabric 4	21"	2"	8	12
Fabric 5	21"	2"	8	12
Fabric 6	21"	2"	8	12
Fabric 7	21"	2"	8	12
Fabric 8	21"	2"	4	6
Border	42"*	4¼"	5	—
	74"**	8¼"	—	4

*Cut strips on crosswise grain.
**Cut strips on lengthwise grain.

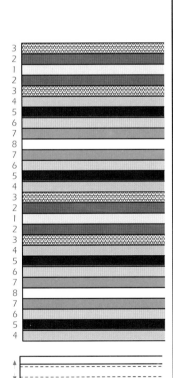

Directions for Crib/Wall Hanging

1. Assign a number to each of the 8 fabrics used and prepare a cutting and sewing guide as shown on page 54.
2. Sew strips together as shown. Make 2 identical units.
3. Press every other seam in the opposite direction, regardless of lightness or darkness of fabric. This will provide for opposing seams when rows are stitched together.
4. Cut sewn strips into 2"-wide units.
5. Arrange units on a flat surface, as shown in the diagram on page 57, so that diagonal bands of color are formed. Do not sew strips together yet! Undo stitching in each row as shown in the diagram, discarding squares from lower corner and 3 units in upper right corner.
6. Position units from the top half below the units in the bottom half. Make sure units are positioned so that diagonal bands of color continue from lower left to upper right. Stitch the units from the upper half to the units in the lower half to complete each row.
7. Sew the vertical rows together, making sure to match the seams between the blocks.
8. To add borders, seam 4¼"-wide border strips as necessary. Measure and stitch borders to sides, then to the top and bottom edges of the quilt top. See pages 77–78.
9. Layer quilt top with batting and backing; baste.
10. Quilt as desired or tie.
11. Bind with bias strips of fabric.

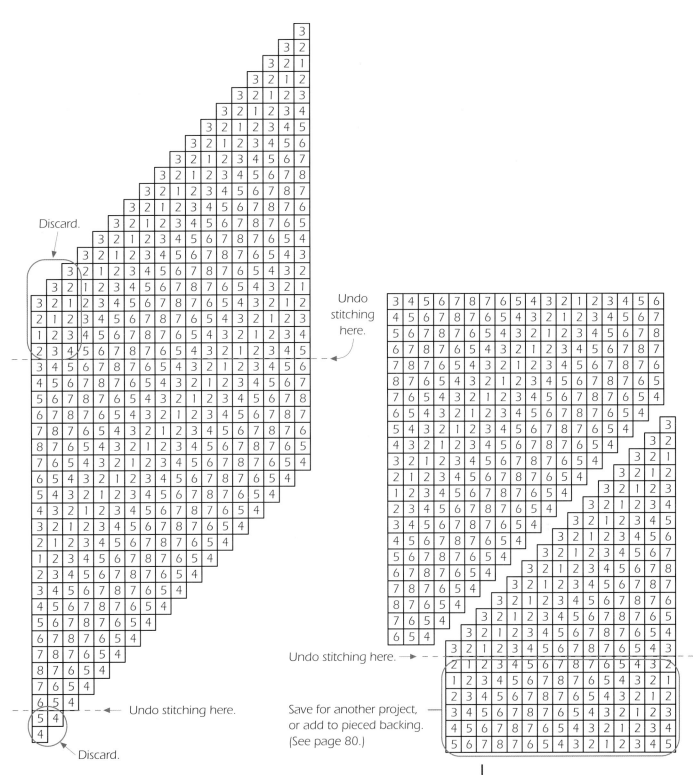

Directions for Twin Size

1. Assign a number to each of the 8 fabrics used and prepare a cutting and sewing guide as shown on page 54.
2. Sew strips together as shown. Make 3 identical units.
3. Press every other seam in the opposite direction, regardless of lightness or darkness of fabric. This will provide for opposing seams when rows are stitched together.
4. Cut sewn strips into 2"-wide units.

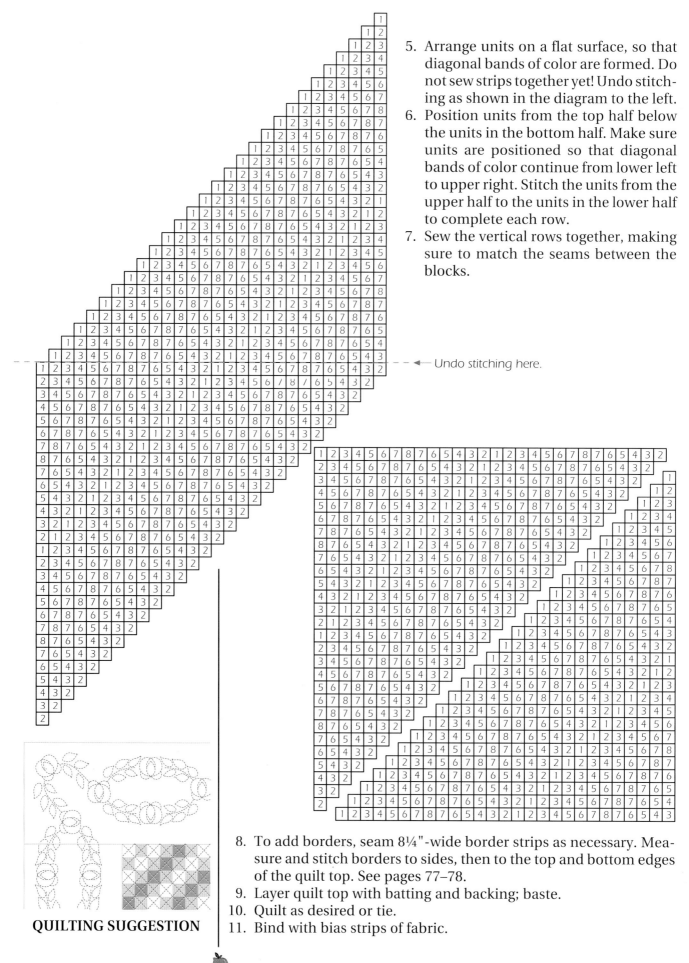

← Undo stitching here.

5. Arrange units on a flat surface, so that diagonal bands of color are formed. Do not sew strips together yet! Undo stitching as shown in the diagram to the left.

6. Position units from the top half below the units in the bottom half. Make sure units are positioned so that diagonal bands of color continue from lower left to upper right. Stitch the units from the upper half to the units in the lower half to complete each row.

7. Sew the vertical rows together, making sure to match the seams between the blocks.

QUILTING SUGGESTION

8. To add borders, seam 8¼"-wide border strips as necessary. Measure and stitch borders to sides, then to the top and bottom edges of the quilt top. See pages 77–78.

9. Layer quilt top with batting and backing; baste.

10. Quilt as desired or tie.

11. Bind with bias strips of fabric.

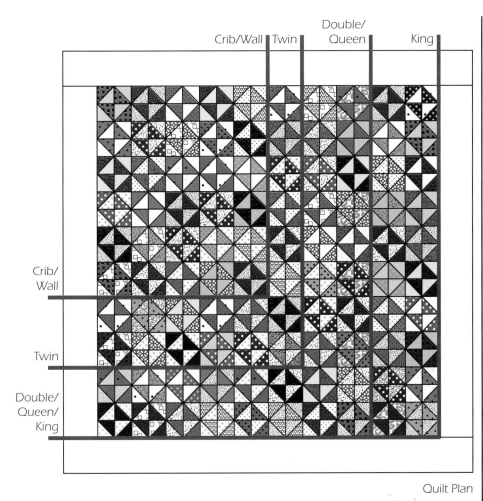

Crib/Wall   Twin   Double/Queen   King

Crib/Wall

Twin

Double/Queen/King

Quilt Plan

Envelope

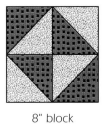

8" block

This traditional pattern resembles the flaps and lines on the back of an envelope, hence its name. The piecing is very similar to the Pinwheel block, and easy, accurate matching is assured if large bias squares are used.

Color photos on pages 32 and 33.

	Crib/Wall	Twin	Dbl/Q	King
Finished Size	48" x 56"	64" x 80"	80" x 96"	96" x 96"
No. of Blocks	30	48	80	100
Block Layout	5 x 6	6 x 8	8 x 10	10 x 10
Border Width	4"	8"	8"	8"

Materials: *44"-wide fabric*

	Crib/Wall	Twin	Dbl/Q	King
Light Fabric	6 fat qtrs.	10 fat qtrs.	16 fat qtrs.	20 fat qtrs.
Dark Fabric	6 fat qtrs.	10 fat qtrs.	16 fat qtrs.	20 fat qtrs.
Border	⅞ yd.	2 yds.	2⅜ yds.	2¾ yds.
Binding	½ yd.	⅝ yd.	¾ yd.	¾ yd.
Backing	2¾ yds.	5½ yds.	5½ yds.	8½ yds.

Cutting

Fabric	Strip Length	Strip Width	Number of Strips			
			Crib/Wall	Twin	Dbl/Q	King
Border	42"	4¼"	6	—	—	—
	42"	8¼"	—	8	10	12

Directions

1. Pair light and dark fat quarters to make bias squares as shown on pages 17–19. Make the first cut 5" from the corner and cut bias strips 3¾" wide. Stitch bias strips together to make pieced fabric. Cut bias squares 4½" x 4½". Cut the number required for the size quilt you are making.

	Crib/Wall	Twin	Dbl/Q	King
4½" Bias Squares	120	192	320	400

2. Stitch bias squares together to make the required number of Envelope blocks. See chart on page 59. Matching bias squares may be used for each block as in Foreign Mail (page 33). Or, you can mix different bias squares for each block as shown in Good Things Come in Small Packages (page 32).
3. Arrange blocks in a pleasing balance of color and print. Sew blocks in horizontal rows. Press seams in opposite directions from row to row. Sew rows together, making sure to match the seams between the blocks. See Tips from the Teacher on page 61.
4. To add borders, seam border strips as necessary. Measure and stitch borders to sides, then to the top and bottom edges of the quilt top. See pages 77–78.
5. Layer quilt top with batting and backing; baste.
6. Quilt as desired or tie.
7. Bind with bias strips of fabric.

Matching Bias Squares Mixed Bias Squares

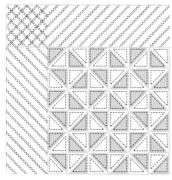

QUILTING SUGGESTION

For hand quilting, quilt ¼" inside all seams. Use angular lines in the border, reversing the directions of the quilting at the center of each border and creating an overlapping grid at the quilt corners. For machine quilting, stitch in the ditch along all the horizontal, vertical, and diagonal lines and continue this grid pattern out into the border.

Envelope

A: Rows of blocks should be pinned together at strategic intersections to ensure accurate matching as rows are sewn together. The process is similar to matching seams within a block.

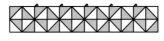
Q: How do I match the rows of blocks while sewing the quilt top together?

To make this process easier, plan for opposing seams when you press blocks after stitching. Press seams in opposite directions from row to row.

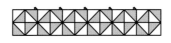

Row 1 — Press seams to right.

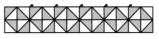

Row 2 — Press seams to left.

Row 3 — Press seams to right.

Carefully matched rows of blocks will meet ¼" from the raw edge when rows are sewn together.

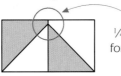

¼" seam allowance for seam intersection

Use positioning pins to hold seam allowances in place. See page 21. Remove pin before stitching through the seam intersection.

Positioning pin   Seam intersection

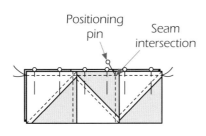

Mock Log Cabin

7½" block for wall hanging
and double/queen
9" block for king

*Based on a ninepatch grid,
this simple block was
inspired by an antique quilt
pictured in Jonathan
Holstein's book,* The Pieced
Quilt. *Select dark and light
shades of the same color
family or choose two
contrasting colors.
Color photos on page 29.*

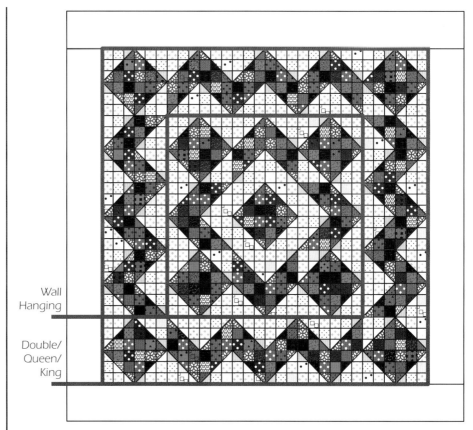

Wall
Hanging

Double/
Queen/
King

Quilt Plan

	Wall Hanging	Dbl/Q	King
Finished Size	45" x 45"	85" x 85"	100" x 100"
Block Size	7½"	7½"	9"
No. of Blocks	36	100	100
Block Layout	6 x 6	10 x 10	10 x 10
Border Width	—	5"	5"

Materials: *44"-wide fabric*

	Wall Hanging	Dbl/Q	King
Light Fabric	7 fat qtrs.	16 fat qtrs.	22 fat qtrs.
Dark Fabric	7 fat qtrs.	16 fat qtrs.	22 fat qtrs.
Border	—	1¼ yds.	1⅞ yds.
Binding	⅜ yd.	¾ yd.	⅞ yd.
Backing	1½ yds.	5 yds.	8½ yds.

Cutting

Cut a 12" or 14" square from each light and dark fat quarter to use in making bias squares. Cut the remaining fat-quarter fabrics into 3" or 3½" squares. See chart below for size and number of squares to cut for the size quilt you are making.

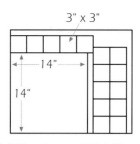

3" x 3"

14"

14"

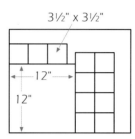

Wall Hanging and Dbl./Queen Cutting Guide

3½" x 3½"

12"

12"

King
Cutting Guide

Fabric	Wall Hanging		Dbl/Q		King	
	No. of Squares	Size	No. of Squares	Size	No. of Squares	Size
Light	7	14" x 14"	16	14" x 14"	22	12" x 12"
	108	3" x 3"	300	3" x 3"	300	3½" x 3½"
Dark	7	14" x 14"	16	14" x 14"	22	12" x 12"
	108	3" x 3"	300	3" x 3"	300	3½" x 3½"

Directions

1. *For wall hanging and double/queen:* To make bias squares, pair the 14" light and dark squares as shown on pages 17–19. Make the first cut 4" from the corner and cut 2¾"-wide bias strips; stitch the strips together. From the pieced fabric, cut 108 bias squares, each 3" x 3" for the wall hanging and 300 bias squares, each 3" x 3" for the double/queen size.

   For king: To make bias squares, pair the 12" light and dark squares as shown on pages 17–19. Make the first cut 4½" from the corner and cut 3"-wide bias strips; stitch the strips together. From the pieced fabric, cut 300 bias squares, each 3½" x 3½".

2. Stitch bias squares, and light and dark squares as shown below to make a Mock Log Cabin block.

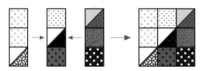

   Make 36 for wall.
   100 for dbl./queen.
   100 for king.

3. Arrange blocks as shown at right for the wall hanging, or as shown on page 64 for the double/queen/king. Stitch blocks in horizontal rows. Press seams in opposite directions from row to row. Stitch rows together, making sure to match the seams between the blocks.

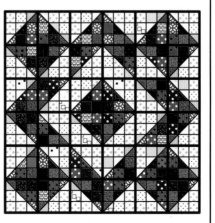

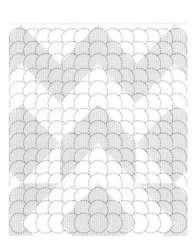

QUILTING SUGGESTION

Begin in the center with a circle. Use a round template to mark arcs or clamshells, which will soften the angular look of this quilt. Continue quilting clamshells out through the border.

4. *For double/queen and king size only:* To add borders, seam 5"-wide border strips as necessary. Measure and stitch borders to sides, then to the top and bottom edges of the quilt top. See pages 77–78.
5. Layer quilt top with batting and backing; baste.
6. Quilt as desired or tie.
7. Bind with bias strips of fabric.

TIPS

from the Teacher

Q: How can I get variety in my bias squares for a scrappy look?

A: Layer 4 fat quarters of fabric in 2 pairs and cut into bias strips. Consult the cutting chart for the quilt you are making to determine strip width and placement of the first cut. See page 18.

Mix and match the cut bias strips from the 4 fabrics to form rectangles and squares. Arrange and sew strips by size, placing the left and lower edges as straight as possible. The remaining edges will most likely be uneven.

   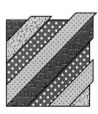

Try pairing 6 different fabrics for greater variety. Just make sure to arrange and sew cut strips into a square or rectangle so there will be little waste.

Twin or Double/Queen   Quilt Plan

Crib/Wall Hanging   Quilt Plan

Delectable Mountains

	Crib/Wall	Twin	Dbl/Q
Finished Size	48" x 48"	72" x 72"	84" x 84"
Block A	4	12	12
Block B	8	12	12
Inner Border	—	3"	3"
Pieced Middle Border	—	2"	2"
Outer Border	4"	4"	10"

Materials: *44"-wide fabric*

	Crib/Wall	Twin	Dbl/Q
Dark Fabric	7 fat qtrs.	12 fat qtrs.	12 fat qtrs.
Light Fabric*	1½ yds.	3 yds.	3 yds.
Inner and Pieced Middle Borders (light)		1⅞ yds.	3⅛ yds.
Outer Border (dark)	⅝ yd.		
Binding	⅜ yd.	½ yd.	⅝ yd.
Backing	2¾ yds.	4½ yds.	4½ yds.

If you want to use different fabrics for the background, purchase fat quarters: 6 for Crib, 8 for Twin, or 8 for Double/Queen.

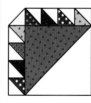

10" Block A

10" Block B

This traditional block and setting uses 2" bias squares for the triangular edges. A single background fabric helps to unify the design. Color photos on page 28.

	Crib/Wall			Twin			Dbl/Q		
	No. of Squares	Size	No. of Triangles	No. of Squares	Size	No. of Triangles	No. of Squares	Size	No. of Triangles
Light Fabric	6	8⅞"	12 ◺	12	8⅞"	24 ◺	12	8⅞"	24 ◺
	4	2⅞"	8 ◿	6	2⅞"	12 ◿	6	2⅞"	12 ◿
Side Triangle	1	12½"	4 ⊠	2	12½"	8 ⊠	2	12½"	8 ⊠
Corner Triangle	2	12¼"	4 ◺	2	12¼"	4 ◺	2	12¼"	4 ◺
Dark Fabric	6	8⅞"	12 ◿	12	8⅞"	24 ◿	12	8⅞"	24 ◿

BORDERS

Fabric	Strip Length	Strip Width	Number of Strips		
			Crib/Wall	Twin	Dbl/Q
Inner Border	42"	3½"	—	8	8
Outer Border	42"	4¼"	5	8	—
		10¼"	—	—	8

Directions

1. To make bias squares, assemble 2 sets of light and dark fat quarters for the crib/wall size, and 6 sets of light and dark fat quarters for the twin and double/queen size. See pages 17–19. From each pair of light and dark fat quarters, make the first cut 4" from the corner and cut 2½"-wide bias strips; stitch the strips together. From the pieced fabrics, cut 100 bias squares, each 2½" x 2½", for the crib/wall size, and 328 bias squares, each 2½" x 2½", for the twin and double/queen. (Reserve 124 bias squares for the pieced middle border on the twin and double/queen.)
2. Sew the light and dark 8⅞" half-square triangles together.
3. Assemble 2½" bias squares and half-square triangle units as shown to make Delectable Mountains blocks A and B.

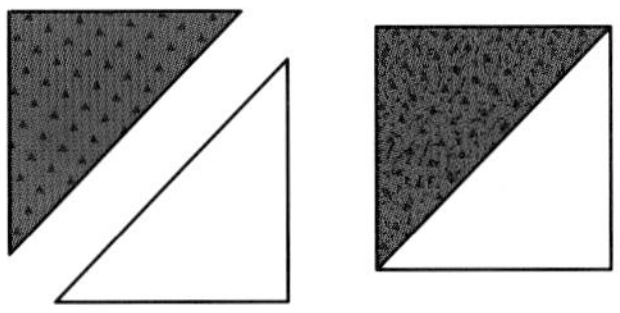

Make 12 (crib).
24 (twin).
24 (dbl./queen).

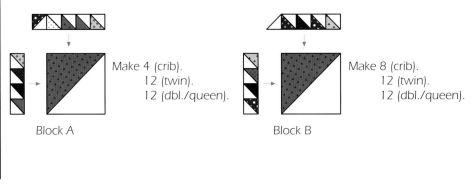

Make 4 (crib).
12 (twin).
12 (dbl./queen).

Make 8 (crib).
12 (twin).
12 (dbl./queen).

Block A

Block B

Quilt Top Assembly and Finishing

1. Arrange blocks in diagonal rows as shown. Add side triangles and corner triangles. Stitch blocks and side triangles in diagonal rows. Press the seams in opposite directions from row to row. Join rows together, making sure to match the seams between the blocks. Sew the corner triangles last. See page 68 for special tips on diagonal settings.

Corner triangle Side triangle

2. Add border for crib/wall size, seaming 4¼"-wide border strips as necessary. Measure and stitch borders to sides, then to the top and bottom edges of the quilt top. See pages 77–78. The crib/wall size does not have a Sawtooth border. If you are making this size, skip to step 5 below.

    Add inner border for twin or double/queen size, seaming 3½"-wide border strips as necessary. Measure and stitch borders to sides, then to the top and bottom edges of the quilt top. See pages 77–78.

3. Add pieced middle border to twin and double/queen size. For side borders, stitch 30 bias squares, 15 facing in each direction as shown. Stitch borders to the sides of the quilt top.

Make 2.

For top and bottom borders, stitch 32 bias squares, 15 facing in each direction, and an additional square at each end, rotated as shown. Stitch borders to the top and bottom of the quilt top. Be sure the end squares are positioned as shown in the quilt plan.

Make 2.

Corner triangle Side triangle

4. Add outer border for twin and double/queen size, seaming 4¼"-wide border strips for the twin or 8¼"-wide border strips for the double/queen as necessary. Measure and stitch borders to sides, then to the top and bottom edges of the quilt top. See pages 77–78.
5. Layer quilt top with batting and backing; baste.
6. Quilt as desired or tie.
7. Bind with bias strips of fabric.

QUILTING SUGGESTION

Quilt diagonal lines from the center of the quilt to the border, 1¼" apart. Quilt a wreath in the center area and a feather design in the inner border. For a simpler quilting design, begin in the center with a circle. Use a round template to mark circles and clamshells from the center out through the border.

TIPS
from the Teacher

Q: How do I accurately make a diagonally set quilt? My tops never seem to lie flat.

A: Diagonally set quilts, such as the Delectable Mountains shown on page 28, are pieced in diagonal rows. Quater-square triangles are used in the corners, and half-square triangles along the outside edges.

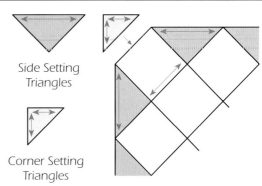

Side Setting Triangles

Corner Setting Triangles

The straight of grain for the side triangles should fall along the outside edge, while the straight of grain for the corner triangles should fall along both outside edges to stabilize the quilt and prevent sagging or ruffled edges. To assure that the straight grain will be placed correctly, cut half-square and quarter-square triangles as shown on pages 12–13. Use the following charts to help compute the correct sizes.*

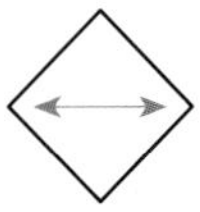

Diagonal Measurements of Standard-Size Blocks

When you set blocks diagonally, it is helpful to know the diagonal measurement of the block so that you can compute the quilt size. To determine this, multiply the length of one side of the block by 1.414 or use the chart at left.

Diagonal Measurement		
2" block	=	2⅞"
3" block	=	4¼"
4" block	=	5⅝"
5" block	=	7⅛"
6" block	=	8½"
7" block	=	9⅞"
8" block	=	11¼"
9" block	=	12¾"
10" block	=	14⅛"
12" block	=	17"
14" block	=	19⅞"
16" block	=	22⅝"
18" block	=	25½"
20" block	=	28¼"
24" block	=	34"

Decimal to Inch Conversions

When you are using a calculator, you will run into fractions given as decimals. Use the chart at right to convert them to fractions or to round them off to the nearest ⅛".

Decimal to Inch		
.125	=	⅛"
.25	=	¼"
.375	=	⅜"
.50	=	½"
.625	=	⅝"
.75	=	¾"
.875	=	⅞"
1.0	=	1"

Corner Triangles

Corner triangles are made from a square cut diagonally in one direction so that one square yields two corner triangles. To calculate the size of the square needed, divide the finished block size by 1.414 and add .875" (⅞") for seam allowances. Round this up to the nearest ⅛".

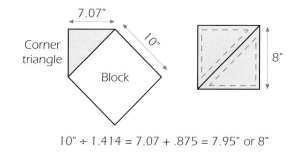

10" ÷ 1.414 = 7.07 + .875 = 7.95" or 8"

Side Triangles

Side triangles are made from a square cut diagonally in two directions so that one square yields four side triangles. To calculate the size of the square needed, multiply the finished block size by 1.414 and add 1.25" (1¼") for seam allowances. Round this up to the nearest ⅛".

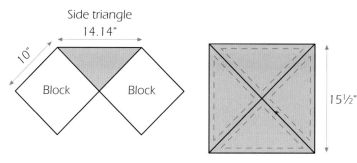

10" x 1.414 = 14.14" + 1.25 = 15.39" or 15½"

The chart at right gives you side and corner triangle measurements for the most common quilt-block sizes. However, you may overcut your squares by ½"–1" and trim them down once your top is pieced together.

Finished Block Size	Cut Square Size for Corner Triangle	Cut Square Size for Side Triangle
2" block	2⅜"	4⅛"
3" block	3"	5½"
4" block	3¾"	7"
5" block	4½"	8⅜"
6" block	5⅛"	9¾"
7" block	5⅞"	11¼"
8" block	6⅝"	12⅝"
9" block	7¼"	14"
10" block	8"	15½"
12" block	9⅜"	18¼"
14" block	10⅞"	21⅛"
16" block	12¼"	23⅞"
18" block	13⅝"	26¾"
20" block	15⅛"	29⅝"
24" block	17⅞"	35¼"

Charts are taken from Sensational Settings by Joan Hanson, a That Patchwork Place book. It is an excellent reference on settings and design.

Indian Trails

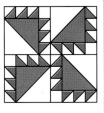

12" block

Based on one of my favorite antique quilts, this traditional pattern is a wonderful choice for a boy's room or any room that calls for a masculine flavor. Select four fabrics: a light background fabric, a dark fabric for the large triangles and border, an accent fabric to use with the light fabric for the bias squares, and a complementary fabric for the alternate blocks. Color photo on page 34.

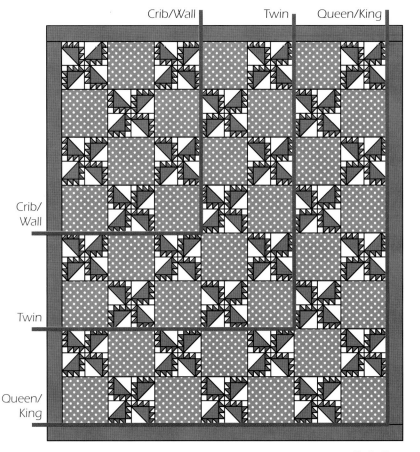

Quilt Plan

	Crib/Wall	Twin	Queen/King
Finished Size	44" x 56"	68" x 92"	92" x 104"
Pieced Block	6	18	28
Alternate Block	6	17	28
Setting	3 x 4	5 x 7	7 x 8
Border Width	4"	4"	4"

Materials: *44"-wide fabric*

	Crib/Wall	Twin	Queen/King
Light Fabric	6 fat qtrs.	9 fat qtrs.	14 fat qtrs.
Accent Fabric	2 fat qtrs.	4 fat qtrs.	6 fat qtrs.
Alternate Block Fabric	¾ yd.	2¼ yds.	3½ yds.
Dark Fabric	1¼ yds.*	2 yds.*	2½ yds.*
Binding	½ yd.	⅝ yd.	¾ yd.
Backing	2½ yds.	4 yds.	8 yds.

Includes yardage for borders.

Cutting

Fabric	Crib/Wall			Twin			Queen/King		
	No. of Squares	Size	No. of Triangles	No. of Squares	Size	No. of Triangles	No. of Squares	Size	No. of Triangles
Light	12	5⅜"	24 △	36	5 ⅜"	72 △	56	5⅜"	112 △
	24	2" x 2"	—	72	2" x 2"	—	112	2" x 2"	—
Dark	12	5⅜"	24 △	36	5⅜"	72 △	56	5⅜"	112 △
Alternate	6	12½" x 12½"	—	17	12½" x 12½"	—	28	12½" x 12½"	—

BORDERS

	Strip Length	Strip Width	Number of Strips		
			Crib/Wall	Twin	Queen/King
Border	42"	4¼"	6	8	10

Directions

1. To make bias squares, assemble sets of light and accent fat quarters as shown on pages 17–19. From each pair of fat quarters, make the first cut 3" from the corner and cut 2" wide bias strips; stitch the strips together. See chart below for the number of light and accent fat-quarter pairs you need, and the number of 2" bias squares required for the size quilt you are making.

	Crib/Wall	Twin	Queen/King
Pairs of Light/Accent FQ	2	4	6
2" x 2" Bias squares	144	432	672

2. Assemble bias squares, 2" squares, and light and dark half-square triangles as shown to make 1 section of the Indian Trails block.

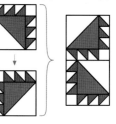

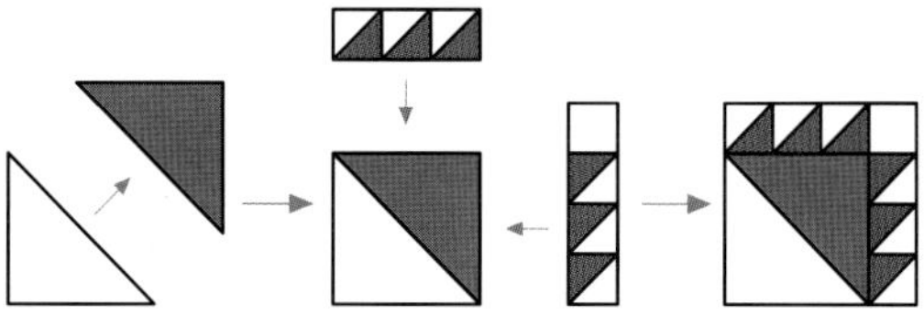

Make 6 (crib).
18 (twin).
28 (queen/king).

3. Join 4 sections to complete the Indian Trails block.

NOTE: Be sure to position the points facing clockwise or counterclockwise within one large block. You can choose to make the Indian Trails with smaller blocks all facing clockwise, or combine the two blocks shown at right to make a variation like the quilt shown on page 34.

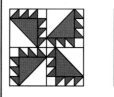

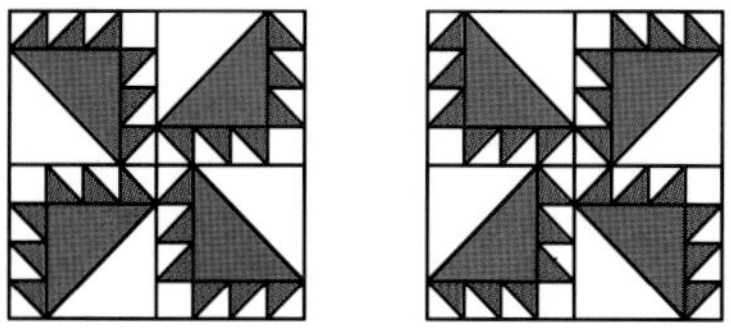

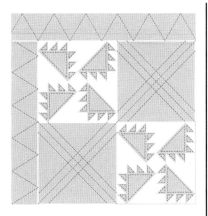

Quilt Top Assembly and Finishing

1. Arrange blocks, alternating Indian Trails blocks and 12½" squares as shown in the quilt plan on page 70. Stitch blocks in horizontal rows. Press seams in opposite directions from row to row. Stitch rows together, making sure to match the seams between the blocks.

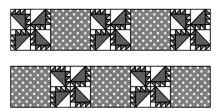

QUILTING SUGGESTION

Quilt ¼" inside all seams on the Indian Trails blocks. Quilt a diagonal design in the alternate blocks and a triangular design in the border.

2. To add borders, seam 4¼"-wide border strips as necessary. Measure and stitch borders to sides, then to the top and bottom edges of the quilt top. See pages 77–78.
3. Layer quilt top with batting and backing; baste.
4. Quilt as desired or tie.
5. Bind with bias strips of fabric.

TIPS

from the Teacher

Q: Is there a trick to making small, accurate bias squares?

A: When making bias squares that finish 1½" or smaller, you will need to press the seams open. This will help to evenly distribute the fabric bulk and avoid lumpy seam intersections, which can pose a real problem when dealing with many small pieces of fabric.

To do so, stitch bias strips with the standard ¼"-wide seam allowances, following the directions on page 17. Place each seam on the ironing board edge as you press to keep previously pressed seams from being disturbed as you press adjacent seams.

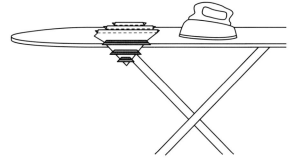

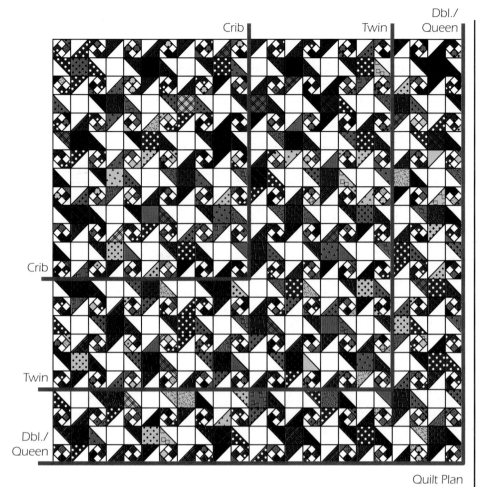

Quilt Plan

Snail's Trail

Unit 1   Unit 3

Unit 2   Unit 4

This traditional pattern is one of many that are not sewn in blocks but as separate units. An allover pattern is created when the units are stitched together. Use a design wall to help you arrange the units to make the Snail's Trail pattern. Tips for creating and using a design wall are found on page 76.

Many color variations are possible for this quilt. The simplest is to use contrasting fabrics. The crib-size quilt on page 35 (bottom) was made using assorted light and dark fat quarters. Light and dark prints are randomly arranged to create the interlocking design.

The variation, Red Snails in the Sunset shown on page 35 (top), uses a single light background fabric combined with many different red prints.

	Crib/Wall	Twin	Dbl/Q
Finished Size	38½" x 45½"	66½" x 66½"	80½" x 80½"
Unit 1	15	40	60
Unit 2	71	180	264
Unit 3	42	100	144
Unit 4	15	41	61

Materials: *44"-wide fabric*

	Crib/Wall	Twin	Dbl/Q
Light Fabric	5 fat qtrs.	12 fat qtrs.	16 fat qtrs.
Dark Fabric	5 fat qtrs.	12 fat qtrs.	16 fat qtrs.
Binding	⅜ yd.	⅝ yd.	¾ yd.
Backing	1½ yds.	3⅞ yds.	4¾ yds.

Cutting

	Crib/Wall			Twin			Dbl/Q		
	No. of Squares	Size	No. of Triangles	No. of Squares	Size	No. of Triangles	No. of Squares	Size	No. of Triangles
Light Fabric									
Unit 3	21	2⅝"	42 ◲	50	2⅝"	100 ◲	72	2⅝"	144 ◲
Unit 2	36	4⅜"	71 ◲	90	4⅜"	180 ◲	132	4⅜"	264 ◲
Unit 1	15	4"	—	40	4"	—	60	4"	—
Dark Fabric									
Unit 3	21	2⅝"	42	50	2⅝"	100	72	2⅝"	144
Unit 2	36	4⅜"	71 ◲	90	4⅜"	180 ◲	132	4⅜"	264 ◲
Unit 4	15	4"	— ◲	41	4"	— ◲	61	4"	— ◲

STRIPS FOR FOUR PATCHES

Fabric	Strip Length	Strip Width	Number of Strips		
			Crib/Wall	Twin	Dbl/Q
Light	21"	1¾"	4	9	12
Dark	21"	1¾"	4	9	12

Directions

Directions are given for creating a scrappy Snail's Trail quilt. Use assorted light and dark fabrics randomly.

UNIT 2

Stitch light and dark 4⅜" half-square triangles together to make Unit 2.

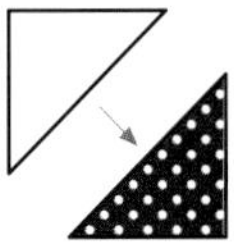

Make 71 (crib/wall).
180 (twin).
264 (dbl./queen).

Unit 2

UNIT 3

1. Sew light and dark strips of fabric together with ¼"-wide seam allowances. Press seam allowances toward the darker fabric.

Make 4 (crib).
9 (twin).
12 (dbl./queen).

2. Layer 2 strip sets together with right sides facing and seam allowances in opposite directions as shown.

3. Cut strip set into 1¾" units, leaving units stacked after cutting.

Cut pairs of units.
42 (crib).
100 (twin).
144 (dbl./queen).

4. Stitch pairs together with ¼"-wide seams. See page 22 for chain-piecing details. Press seam to one side.

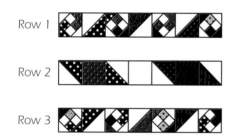

Make 42 (crib).
100 (twin).
144 (dbl./queen).

5. Position Four Patch as shown in diagram. Stitch 2 light 2⅝" half-square triangles to the upper right and lower left sides as shown. Press seams toward corners.

Make 42 (crib).
100 (twin).
144 (dbl./queen).

6. Stitch 2 dark 2⅝" half-square triangles to the remaining sides of the Four Patch as shown to complete Unit 3. Press seams toward corners.

Make 42 (crib).
100 (twin).
144 (dbl./queen).

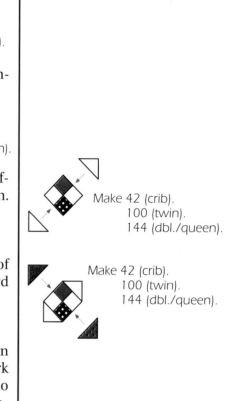

7. Using a design wall, arrange Units 1, 2, 3, and 4 into rows as shown in the quilt plan on page 73. Rotate the units so that all of the dark fabrics make one interlocking design and all of the light fabrics do likewise. Be careful as you place Units 2 and 3, since the placement of the light and dark triangles vary within each row.

Row 1

Row 2

Row 3

Mark the left side of each row with a pin. This will help when stitching rows together. It is easy to lose track of the pattern and turn a row wrong side up. Keeping all the pins at the left side of the quilt will help to sew rows correctly. It is also helpful to label rows with paper labels so rows will be sewn to each other in the correct order.

8. Stitch units into horizontal rows. Press seams in opposite directions from row to row. Stitch rows together, making sure to match the seams between the blocks.
9. Layer quilt top with batting and backing; baste.
10. Quilt as desired or tie.
11. Bind with bias strips of fabric.

QUILTING SUGGESTION

Quilt in-the-ditch around the snail shape.

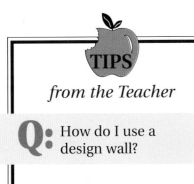

Q: How do I use a design wall?

A: Design walls are used to test, vary, and evaluate color and fabric placement before the quilt blocks are stitched together. In its simplest form, a design wall is a large, flat area with a surface to which fabrics adhere without pinning.

Design walls can be easily created from materials on hand. Try one of the following variations:

1. Stitch a casing to one edge of a flannel sheet. Slip a dowel through the casing and mount on the wall.
2. Pin a piece of Pellon Fleece™, Thermolan™, or Warm and Natural™ batting to a wall or bulletin board.
3. Cover a 4' x 6' piece of foam core board with a flannel sheet and secure to the wall.
4. Use a folding screen with a textured surface so fabrics may be pinned to it.

To use a design wall, simply press your fabric pieces against the surface, causing the fabric to adhere. Fabric pieces can be moved easily from one area to another to try different arrangements. It may be necessary to pin rows of blocks to the design wall because of their weight.

Use a Polaroid camera to help evaluate and record designs as you vary the placement of fabric. It will be easier to re-create an earlier design possibility if you have a photograph to guide you. A picture is also a lifesaver if the fabrics on your design wall are disturbed or fall.

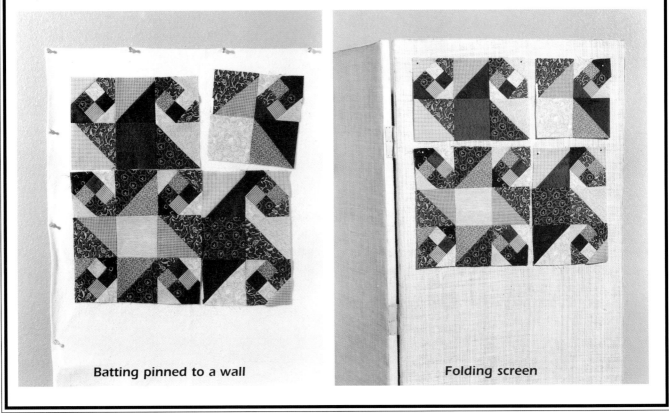

Batting pinned to a wall   **Folding screen**

Adding Borders

The edges of a quilt should be straightened before the borders are added. There should be little or no trimming needed for a straight-set quilt.

To find the correct measurement for straight-cut border strips, always measure through the center of the quilt, not at the outside edges. This ensures that the borders are of equal length on opposite sides of the quilt and brings the outer edges into line with the center dimension if discrepancies exist. Otherwise, your quilt might not be "square" due to minor piecing discrepancies and/or stretching that can occur while you work with the pieces. If there is a large difference in the two sides, it is better to go back and correct the source of the problem rather than try to make the border fit and end up with a distorted quilt.

The easiest border to add is a straight-cut border. This method has been used on all the quilts with borders in this book. You will save fabric if you attach the border to the longest sides first, then stitch the border to the remaining two sides.

1. Measure the length of the quilt at the center. Cut two of the border strips to this measurement.

If borders have been cut on the crosswise grain, you may need to piece strips together before adding them to the quilt. The seam will be less noticeable and stronger if pieced on an angle.

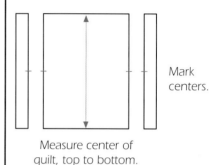

Measure center of quilt, top to bottom.

Mark centers.

Draw a line between overhanging fabric edge, then stitch.

Finished angled seam

Mark the centers of the border strips and the quilt top. Pin borders to the sides of the quilt, matching centers and ends and easing or slightly stretching the quilt to fit the border strip as necessary.

TIPS

from the Teacher

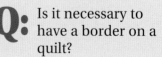

Q: Is it necessary to have a border on a quilt?

A: It isn't always necessary to have a border on a quilt. Many of the antique quilts made from scraps have no border, since continuous yardage was scarce and expensive. Bright Lights and Vintage Barn Raising (page 31), Pinwheel Squares and Pretty in Pink (page 36), Red Snails in the Sunset and Ancient Snails (page 35) and Liberty on the Loose (page 29) are examples of quilts without borders.

Borders can be used to frame and soften a busy design. They are also helpful in enlarging a quilt to fit a standard-size bed. You'll notice that some of the quilt plans call for the same number of blocks when making two different size quilts. The larger size quilt has a border, while the smaller does not.

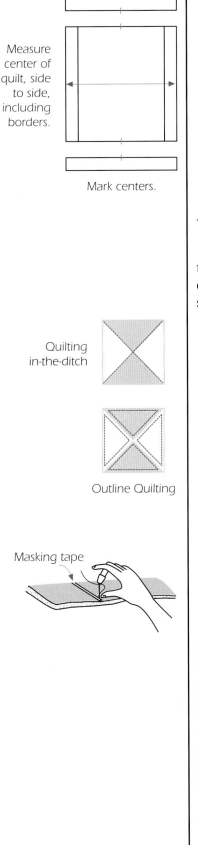

Measure center of quilt, side to side, including borders.

Mark centers.

Quilting in-the-ditch

Outline Quilting

Masking tape

2. Sew the side borders in place and press the seams toward the borders.
3. Measure the center width of the quilt, including the side borders, to determine the length of the top and bottom border. Cut the border strips to this measurement, piecing strips as necessary. Mark the centers of the border strips and the quilt top. Pin borders to the top and bottom of the quilt top, easing or slightly stretching the quilt to fit as necessary.
4. Sew the top and bottom borders in place and press the seams toward the borders.

Marking the Quilting Design

Whether you machine or hand quilt, you'll need to mark a design to be quilted on the quilt top unless you are stitching in-the-ditch, outlining the design ¼" away from all seams, or stitching a grid of straight lines, using ¼"-wide masking tape as a guide.

1. To stitch in-the-ditch, place the stitches in the valley created next to the seam. Stitch on the side that does not have the seam allowance under it.
2. To outline a design, stitch ¼" away from the seam inside each shape.
3. To mark a grid or pattern of lines, use ¼"-wide masking tape in 15" to 18" lengths. Place strips of tape on a small area and quilt next to the edge of the tape. Remove tape when stitching is complete. Tape can be reused to mark another area.

CAUTION: Don't leave tape on quilt top for any extended length of time; it may leave a sticky residue.

To mark more intricate designs, use a stencil or a light table. Quilting stencils made from durable plastic are available in quilt shops. Use stencils to mark repeated designs. There is a groove cut into the plastic, wide enough to allow the use of a marking device or pen. Just place the marker inside the groove to quickly transfer the design on the fabric. Good marking pens or pencils that are removable or can be washed out are Berol silver pencils, EZ Washout marking pencils, mechanical pencils, or sharp regular pencils. Just be sure to draw lines lightly. Always test any marking device for removability on a scrap of fabric.

Use a light table to trace more intricate designs from books containing quilting patterns.

To make your own light table:

Separate your dining-room table as if adding an extra leaf. Then place a piece of glass, plastic, or Plexiglas over the opening. (I use the removable glass from a storm door for safety's sake because there is a frame around the edge of the glass.) Have the glass (or glass substitute) cut to fit your table at a glass shop, if desired, and frame or tape the edges to avoid cut fingers. For an additional fee, you can have glass edges finished to eliminate the sharp edges.

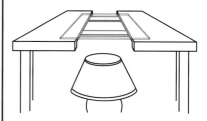

Once the glass is in place, position a table lamp on the floor beneath it, and you have an instant light table. If your table does not separate, two card tables or end tables of the same height can be pushed together to create a support for the glass.

Backing

If you use 42"-wide fabric, you will need to piece together the backing from two or more strips of fabric for most quilts larger than crib size. The seams can run horizontally or vertically in a pieced backing, as long as the fabric isn't a directional print. Avoid the temptation to use a bed sheet for a backing as it is difficult to quilt through. Cut backing 3"–4" larger than the quilt top all around.

Plan to put a sleeve or rod pocket on the back of the quilt so it can be hung. See pages 86–87. Purchase extra backing fabric so that the sleeve and the backing match. Once you know the finished size of your quilt, refer to the following diagrams to plan the backing layout and to determine how much fabric you'll need. Be sure to trim off the selvages where pieces are joined.

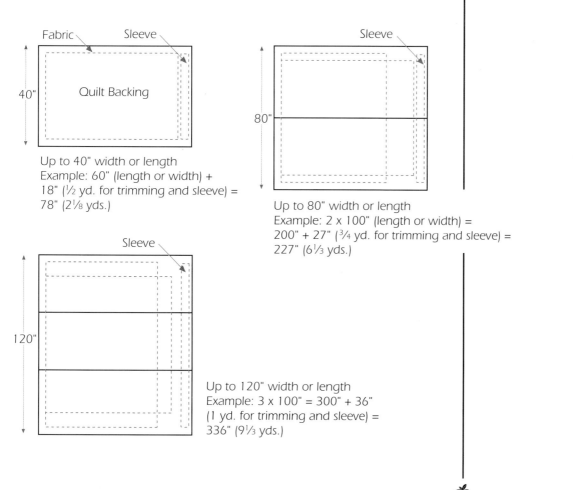

Up to 40" width or length
Example: 60" (length or width) + 18" (½ yd. for trimming and sleeve) = 78" (2⅛ yds.)

Up to 80" width or length
Example: 2 x 100" (length or width) = 200" + 27" (¾ yd. for trimming and sleeve) = 227" (6⅓ yds.)

Up to 120" width or length
Example: 3 x 100" = 300" + 36" (1 yd. for trimming and sleeve) = 336" (9⅓ yds.)

TIPS
from the Teacher

Q: Suppose my backing is just a little too narrow for a 45"-wide quilt. Do I have to buy twice the amount of fabric?

A: Pieced backs are fun to make and they can be the answer to this annoying problem. Several innovative solutions are shown on page 26.

The navy blue checked backing was just slightly too narrow, so I trimmed a 6" strip from one lengthwise edge. I then took leftover segments, bias squares, and partial blocks from the quilt front and pieced a 4"-wide strip. I stitched this pieced strip between the two sections of navy blue checked fabric, giving the backing a decorative touch while solving a problem.

You can also use different scraps of fabric from your sewing stash, piecing them together to form a piece of fabric large enough for a backing. This is most effective when you use some of the fabrics that were used on the front of the quilt. The photo on page 26 also shows the back of Straight and Narrow and the brightly colored back of Bright Lights, both made by piecing remaining fat-quarter fabrics.

Batting

There are many types of batting to choose from. Select a high-loft batting for a bed quilt that you want to look puffy. Lightweight battings are fine for baby quilts or wall hangings. A lightweight batting is easier to quilt through and shows the quilting design well. It also has an old-fashioned look, resembling antique quilts.

Polyester batting works well, doesn't shift after washing, and is easy to quilt through. It comes in lightweight and regular lofts as well as a fat batting or high loft for comforters.

Cotton batting is a good choice if you are quilting an old quilt top. This batting must be quilted with stitches no more than 2" apart.

Dark batting works well behind a dark quilt top. If there is any bearding (batting fibers creeping through the top), it will not be as noticeable.

Layering and Basting

Open a package of batting and smooth it out flat. Allow batting to rest in this position for at least twenty-four hours. Press backing so that all seams are flat and the fold lines have been removed.

A large dining room table, ping pong table, or two large folding tables pushed together make an ideal work surface on which to prepare your quilt. Use a table pad to protect your dining-room table. The floor is not a good choice for layering your quilt. It requires too much bending, and the layers can easily shift or be disturbed.

Place the backing on the table with the wrong side of the fabric facing up. If the table is large enough, you may want to tape the backing down with masking tape. Spread your batting over the backing, centering it, and smooth out any remaining folds.

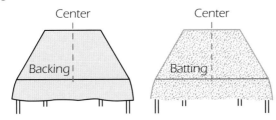

Center the freshly pressed and marked quilt top on these two layers. Check all four sides to make sure there is adequate batting and backing. Stretch backing to make sure it is still smooth.

The basting method you use depends on whether you will be hand quilting or machine quilting. Safety-pin basting is generally used for machine quilting, while thread basting is used for hand quilting.

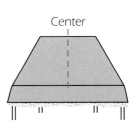

Thread Basting

Starting in the middle, baste the three layers together with straight pins while gently smoothing out the fullness to the sides and corners. Take care not to distort the straight lines of the quilt design and the borders.

After pinning, baste the layers together with a needle and light-colored thread. Start in the middle and make a line of long stitches to each corner to form a large X. Continue basting in a grid of parallel lines 6"–8" apart. Finish with a row of basting around the outside edges. Quilts that are to be quilted with a hoop or on your lap will be handled more than those quilted on a frame; therefore, they will require more basting. After basting, remove the pins. Now you are ready to quilt.

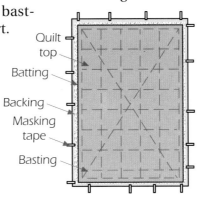

Quilt top
Batting
Backing
Masking tape
Basting

Pin Basting

A quick way to baste a quilt top is with size 2 safety pins. They are large enough to catch all three layers but not so large that they will snag fine fabric. Begin pinning in the center and work out toward the edges. Place pins 4"–5" apart.

Use long straight pins along the outside edge to hold everything in place. Place pins perpendicular to the edge, 1½"–2" apart.

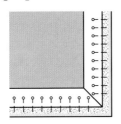

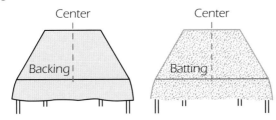

Safety-pin basting

Hand Quilting

To quilt by hand, you will need quilting thread, quilting needles, small scissors, a thimble, and perhaps a balloon or large rubber band to help grasp the needle if it gets stuck. Quilt on a frame, a large hoop, or just on your lap or a table. Use a single strand of quilting thread not longer than 18". Make a small, single knot in the end of the thread. The quilting stitch is a small running stitch that goes through all three layers of the quilt. Take two, three, or even four stitches at a time if you can keep them even. When crossing seams, you might find it necessary to "hunt and peck" one stitch at a time.

To begin, insert the needle in the top layer about ¾" from the point you want to start stitching. Pull the needle out at the starting point and gently tug at the knot until it pops through the fabric and is buried in the batting. Make a backstitch and begin quilting. Stitches should be tiny (8–10 per inch is good), even, and straight; tiny will come with practice.

When you come almost to the end of the thread, make a single knot ¼" from the fabric. Take a backstitch to bury the knot in the batting. Run the thread off through the batting and out the quilt top; snip it off. The first and last stitches will look different from the running stitches in between. To make them less noticeable, start and stop where quilting lines cross each other or at seam joints.

Hand quilting stitch

Machine Quilting

Machine quilting is a good choice for those who have little time and need to finish their tops in a hurry. It's also a very practical choice for baby quilts or other items that will need lots of washing.

Machine quilting works best on small projects; it can be frustrating to feed the bulk of a large quilt through the machine.

Use a walking foot or even-feed foot (or the built-in, even-feed feature, when available) for your sewing machine to help the quilt layers feed through the machine without shifting or puckering. This type of foot is essential for straight-line and grid quilting and for large, simple curves. Read the machine instruction manual for special tension settings to sew through extra fabric thicknesses.

Curved designs require free fabric movement under the foot of the sewing machine. This is called free-motion quilting, and with a little practice, you can imitate beautiful hand quilting designs quickly. If you wish to do curved quilting designs with your machine, use a darning foot and lower the feed dog while using this foot. Because the feed dog is lowered for free-motion quilting, the speed that you run the machine and feed the fabric under the foot determines the stitch length. Practice running the machine fairly fast, since this makes it easier to sew smoother lines of quilting. With free-motion quilting, do not turn the fabric under the needle. Instead, guide the fabric as if it were under a stationary pencil (the needle).

Practice first on a piece of fabric until you get the feel of controlling the motion of the fabric with your hands. Stitch some free-form scribbles, zigzags, and curves. Try a heart or a star. Then, practice on a

Walking foot attachment

Darning foot

A: Comforters can be made by tacking or tying the quilt top. Often the yarn, ribbon, or buttons used to tack or tie a quilt provides an additional source of decoration.

from the Teacher

Q: Must I quilt my top? Are there other ways to finish it?

sample block with batting and backing. Make sure your chair is adjusted to a comfortable height. At first, this type of quilting may feel a bit awkward, but with a little determination and practice, you will have the satisfaction of being able to complete a project with beautiful machine quilting in a few hours.

Keep the spacing between quilting lines consistent over the entire quilt. Avoid using complex, little designs and leaving large unquilted spaces. For most battings, a 2" or 3" square is the largest area that can be left unquilted. Read the instructions enclosed with the batting you have chosen.

Do not try to machine quilt an entire quilt in one sitting, even if it's a small quilt. Break the work into short periods; stretch and relax your muscles regularly.

When all the quilting is completed, remove the safety pins. Sometimes it will be necessary to remove safety pins as you work.

Tying

To prepare a quilt for tying, cut the backing to match the top. Place the top and backing with right sides together and stitch on three sides, using a ¼"-wide seam allowance. On the fourth unsewn side, press the raw edge under ¼". Lay the quilt on a flat surface with the wrong side of the pieced top up. Lay the batting on the quilt top and baste it to the seam allowance with needle and thread. Trim excess batting. Turn the whole thing right side out as you would a pillowcase. Smooth it out and pin-baste the three layers along the side seams. This will help keep the comforter flat and the side seams from rolling to the front or back. Pin the unsewn end closed, using the pressed creases as a guide. Then, place pins at every point you want to locate a tie.

Don't leave more than 5"–7" unsecured. Ties can be placed at the corners and center of each block and along the middle of each border. Tie to the front or back of the comforter. Ties on the back don't interfere visually with the pieced design on the front.

To tie a top, use a large, sharp needle and sportweight yarn or pearl cotton. Cut a long (2'–3') piece of yarn. Double it if the thread is very thin. Make a stitch where the first tie will be. Don't cut the yarn yet, but skip over and make a stitch at the next location, and so on, until you run out of yarn in your needle.

Place pins along edges first to stabilize side seams. Then put a pin in each place you want to put a tie.

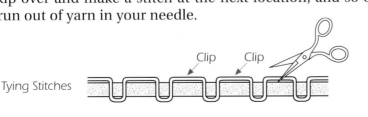

Clip   Clip

Tying Stitches

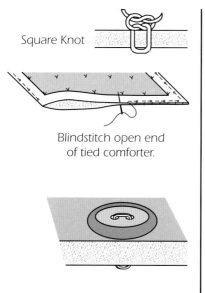

Square Knot

Blindstitch open end of tied comforter.

Snip the yarn between the stitches and make the ties. Tie square knots (right over left and left over right).

Trim ties to about 1" or 1½" long. After tying, close the open end of the comforter by hand, using a blind stitch.

Tacking with Buttons

To use buttons as shown in the detail of the Spool quilt by Joan Hanson (shown below), lower the feed dog on the machine and set the stitch length at 0. Adjust the stitch width to match the holes in each button. Stitch buttons, tacking through all three layers. Buttons should not be used on quilts for young children since they can be pulled off.

Bartacking with Ribbon

Cut an 8" length of ⅛"-wide ribbon and fold in half. Place fold on area to be tacked. Stitch a bartack (a wide stitch over the same position usually 6 or 7 times) over the center of the ribbon, securing it to the comforter. Tie the ends of the ribbon into bows.

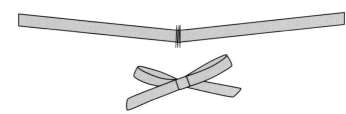

Binding the Edges

My favorite quilt binding is a double-layer French binding made from bias strips. It rolls over the edges nicely, and the two layers of fabric resist wear. If you use 2¼"-wide strips, the finished width of this binding will be ⅜".

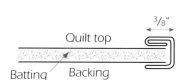

³/₈"

Quilt top

Batting   Backing

Double-Layer French Binding

Finishing Techniques

The quilt directions tell you how much fabric to purchase for binding. However, if you enlarge your quilt or need to compute binding fabric, use this handy chart:

Length of binding	Fabric needed
115"	¼ yd.*
180"	⅜ yd.
255"	½ yd.
320"	⅝ yd.
400"	¾ yd.
465"	⅞ yd.

It is a good idea to purchase ½ yard of fabric instead of ¼ yard so the bias strips will be longer and the continuous binding won't have as many seams.

Determine the distance around your quilt and add about 20" for turning the corners and for seaming the binding strips together into one continuous piece.

After quilting, trim excess batting and backing even with the edge of the quilt top. A rotary cutter and long ruler will ensure accurate straight edges. If basting is no longer in place, baste all three layers together. If you intend to attach a sleeve or rod pocket, make one now. See pages 86–87.

1. Cut 2¼"-wide bias strips as shown on page 16.
2. Stitch bias strips together, offsetting them as shown. Press seams open.

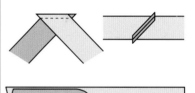

3. Fold the strip in half lengthwise, wrong sides together, and press.

4. Unfold binding at one end and turn under ¼" at a 45° angle as shown.

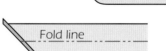

Fold line

5. Beginning on one side of the quilt, stitch the binding to the quilt, using a ¼"-wide seam allowance. Start stitching 1"–2" from the start of the binding. Stop stitching ¼" from the corner and backstitch.

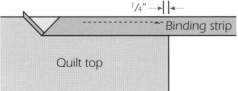

¼" →||←
--------- Binding strip

Quilt top

6. Turn the quilt to prepare for sewing along the next edge. Fold the binding away from the quilt as shown, then fold again to place binding along second edge of the quilt. (This fold creates an angled pleat at the corner.)

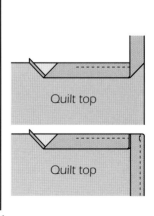

Quilt top

Quilt top

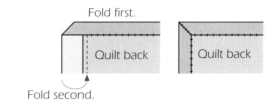

7. Stitch from the fold of the binding along the second edge of the quilt top, stopping ¼" from the corner as you did for the first corner; backstitch. Repeat stitching and mitering process on remaining edges and corners of the quilt.

8. When you reach the beginning of the binding, cut the end 1" longer than needed and tuck the end inside the beginning.

9. Turn binding to the back side, over the raw edges of the quilt and blindstitch in place, with the folded edge covering the row of machine stitching. At each corner, fold binding as shown to form a miter on the back of the quilt.

Fold first.

Quilt back   Quilt back

Fold second.

Quilt Labels

It's a good idea to label a quilt with its name, the name and address of the maker, and the date on which it was made. Include the name of the quilter(s) if the quilt was quilted by a group or someone other than the maker. On an antique quilt, record all the information that you know about the quilt, including where you purchased it. If the quilt is being presented to someone as a gift, also include that information.

To easily make a label, use a permanent pen to print or legibly write all this information on a piece of muslin. Press freezer paper to the back of the muslin to stabilize it while writing. Press raw edges to the wrong side of the label. Remove freezer paper and stitch securely to the lower corner of the quilt. You can also do labels in cross-stitch or embroidery.

Quilt Sleeves

If you plan to hang your quilt, attach a sleeve or rod pocket to the back before you attach the binding. From the leftover backing fabric, cut an 8"-wide strip of fabric equal to the width of your quilt. You may need to piece two or three strips together for larger quilts. On each end, fold over ½" and then fold ½" again. Press and stitch by machine.

½"   ½"

Fold the strip in half lengthwise, wrong sides together; baste the raw edges to the top edge of the back of your quilt. These will be secured when you sew on the binding. Your quilt should be about 1" wider than the sleeve on both sides. Make a little pleat in the sleeve to accommodate the thickness of the rod and then slipstitch the ends and bottom edge of the sleeve to the backing fabric. This keeps the rod from being inserted next to the quilt backing.

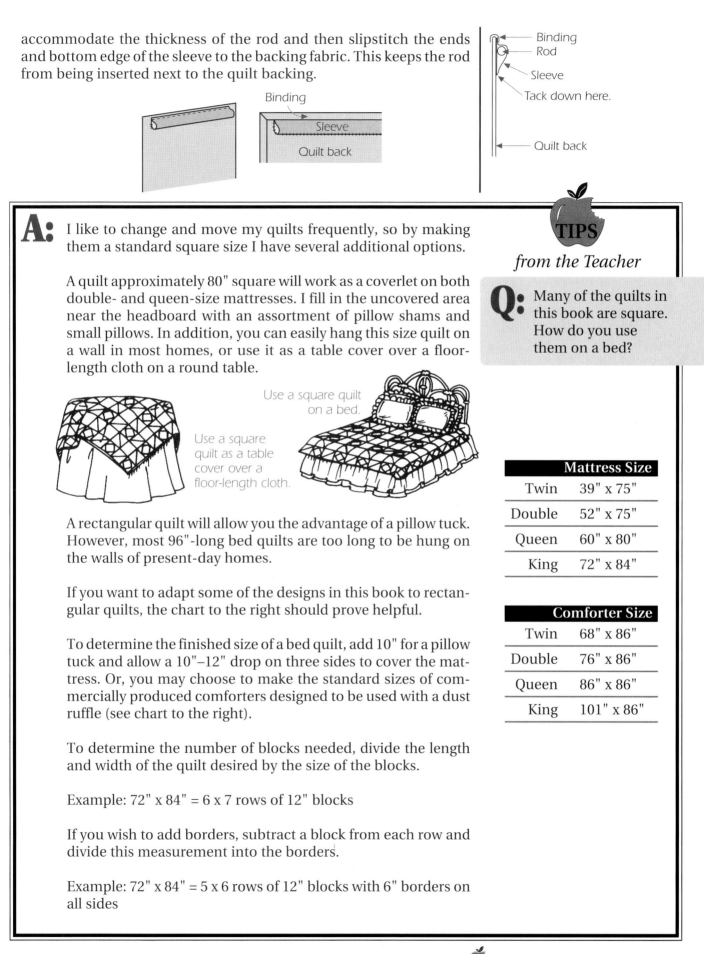

Binding

Binding
Sleeve
Quilt back

Binding
Rod
Sleeve
Tack down here.
Quilt back

A: I like to change and move my quilts frequently, so by making them a standard square size I have several additional options.

A quilt approximately 80" square will work as a coverlet on both double- and queen-size mattresses. I fill in the uncovered area near the headboard with an assortment of pillow shams and small pillows. In addition, you can easily hang this size quilt on a wall in most homes, or use it as a table cover over a floor-length cloth on a round table.

Use a square quilt on a bed.

Use a square quilt as a table cover over a floor-length cloth.

TIPS from the Teacher

Q: Many of the quilts in this book are square. How do you use them on a bed?

A rectangular quilt will allow you the advantage of a pillow tuck. However, most 96"-long bed quilts are too long to be hung on the walls of present-day homes.

If you want to adapt some of the designs in this book to rectangular quilts, the chart to the right should prove helpful.

To determine the finished size of a bed quilt, add 10" for a pillow tuck and allow a 10"–12" drop on three sides to cover the mattress. Or, you may choose to make the standard sizes of commercially produced comforters designed to be used with a dust ruffle (see chart to the right).

To determine the number of blocks needed, divide the length and width of the quilt desired by the size of the blocks.

Example: 72" x 84" = 6 x 7 rows of 12" blocks

If you wish to add borders, subtract a block from each row and divide this measurement into the borders.

Example: 72" x 84" = 5 x 6 rows of 12" blocks with 6" borders on all sides

Mattress Size	
Twin	39" x 75"
Double	52" x 75"
Queen	60" x 80"
King	72" x 84"

Comforter Size	
Twin	68" x 86"
Double	76" x 86"
Queen	86" x 86"
King	101" x 86"

That Patchwork Place Publications and Products

BOOKS

Angle Antics by Mary Hickey
Animas Quilts by Jackie Robinson
Appliqué Borders: An Added Grace by Jeana Kimball
Baltimore Bouquets by Mimi Dietrich
Basket Garden by Mary Hickey
Biblical Blocks by Rosemary Makhan
Blockbuster Quilts by Margaret J. Miller
Calendar Quilts by Joan Hanson
Cathedral Window: A Fresh Look by Nancy J. Martin
Corners in the Cabin by Paulette Peters
Country Medallion Sampler by Carol Doak
Country Threads by Connie Tesene and Mary Tendall
Easy Machine Paper Piecing by Carol Doak
Even More by Trudie Hughes
Fantasy Flowers: Pieced Flowers for Quilters
    by Doreen Cronkite Burbank
Feathered Star Sampler by Marsha McCloskey
Fit To Be Tied by Judy Hopkins
Five- and Seven-Patch Blocks & Quilts for the ScrapSaver™
    by Judy Hopkins
Four-Patch Blocks & Quilts for the ScrapSaver™
    by Judy Hopkins
Fun with Fat Quarters by Nancy J. Martin
Go Wild with Quilts: 14 North American Birds and Animals
    by Margaret Rolfe
Handmade Quilts by Mimi Dietrich
Happy Endings—Finishing the Edges of Your Quilt
    by Mimi Dietrich
Holiday Happenings by Christal Carter
Home for Christmas by Nancy J. Martin and Sharon Stanley
In The Beginning by Sharon Evans Yenter
Jacket Jazz by Judy Murrah
Lessons in Machine Piecing by Marsha McCloskey
Little By Little: Quilts in Miniature by Mary Hickey
Little Quilts by Alice Berg, Sylvia Johnson, and
    Mary Ellen Von Holt
Lively Little Logs by Donna McConnell
Loving Stitches: A Guide to Fine Hand Quilting
    by Jeana Kimball
More Template-Free™ *Quiltmaking* by Trudie Hughes
Nifty Ninepatches by Carolann M. Palmer
Nine-Patch Blocks & Quilts for the ScrapSaver™
    by Judy Hopkins
Not Just Quilts by Jo Parrott
On to Square Two by Marsha McCloskey
Osage County Quilt Factory by Virginia Robertson
Painless Borders by Sally Schneider
A Perfect Match: A Guide to Precise Machine Piecing
    by Donna Lynn Thomas

Picture Perfect Patchwork by Naomi Norman
Piecemakers® *Country Store* by the Piecemakers
Pineapple Passion by Nancy Smith and Lynda Milligan
A Pioneer Doll and Her Quilts by Mary Hickey
Pioneer Storybook Quilts by Mary Hickey
Quick & Easy Quiltmaking: 26 Projects Featuring Speedy
    Cutting and Piecing Methods by Mary Hickey,
    Nancy J. Martin, Marsha McCloskey & Sara Nephew
Quilts for All Seasons: Year-Round Log Cabin Designs
    by Christal Carter
Quilts for Baby: Easy as A, B, C by Ursula Reikes
Quilts for Kids by Carolann M. Palmer
Quilts from Nature by Joan Colvin
Quilts to Share by Janet Kime
Red and Green: An Appliqué Tradition by Jeana Kimball
Red Wagon Originals by Gerry Kimmel and Linda Brannock
Rotary Riot: 40 Fast & Fabulous Quilts by Judy Hopkins
    and Nancy J. Martin
Rotary Roundup: 40 More Fast & Fabulous Quilts by Judy
    Hopkins and Nancy J. Martin
Samplings from the Sea by Rosemary Makhan
Scrap Happy by Sally Schneider
Sensational Settings: Over 80 Ways to Arrange Your Quilt
    Blocks by Joan Hanson
Sewing on the Line: Fast and Easy Foundation Piecing
    by Lesly-Claire Greenberg
Shortcuts: A Concise Guide to Rotary Cutting
    by Donna Lynn Thomas (metric version available)
Small Talk by Donna Lynn Thomas
Smoothstitch™ *Quilts: Easy Machine Appliqué*
    by Roxi Eppler
The Stitchin' Post by Jean Wells and Lawry Thorn
Strips That Sizzle by Margaret J. Miller
Tea Party Time: Romantic Quilts and Tasty Tidbits
    by Nancy J. Martin
Template-Free™ *Quiltmaking* by Trudie Hughes
Template-Free™ *Quilts and Borders* by Trudie Hughes
Template-Free® *Stars* by Jo Parrott
Watercolor Quilts by Pat Maixner Magaret and
    Donna Ingram Slusser
Women and Their Quilts by Nancyann Johanson Twelker

TOOLS

6" Bias Square®   Rotary Mate™
8" Bias Square®   Rotary Rule™
Metric Bias Square®   Ruby Beholder™
BiRangle™   ScrapSaver™
Pineapple Rule

VIDEO

Shortcuts to America's Best-Loved Quilts

Many titles are available at your local quilt shop. For more information, send $2 for a color catalog to That Patchwork Place, Inc., PO Box 118, Bothell WA 98041-0118 USA.

☎ Call 1-800-426-3126 for the name and location of the quilt shop nearest you.